D1521144

Decision Making in
Child Welfare Services

INTERNATIONAL SERIES
IN SOCIAL WELFARE

Decision Making in Child Welfare Services

Intake and Planning

Theodore J. Stein
New York University
School of Social Work

Tina L. Rzepnicki
Fordham University
Graduate School of Social Service

Kluwer-Nijhoff Publishing
A member of the Kluwer Academic Publishers Group
Boston/The Hague/Dordrecht/Lancaster

Distributors for North America:
Kluwer Boston, Inc.
190 Old Derby Street
Hingham, MA 02043, U.S.A.

Distributors Outside North America:
Kluwer Academic Publishers Group
Distribution Centre
P. O. Box 322
3300AH Dordrecht, The Netherlands

Library of Congress Cataloging in Publication Data
Stein, Theodore J.
  Decision making in child welfare services.

  (International series in social welfare)
  Includes bibliographical references and indexes.
    1. Child welfare—United States—Decision making.
  2. Social work with children—United States—Decision making.
  3. Adoption—United States—Decision making.   4. Foster home care
  —United States—Decision making.
  I. Rzepnicki, Tina L.   II. Title.   III. Series.
  HV741.S7442   1984   362.7'95'068   83-12006
  ISBN 0-89838-138-X

Printed in the United States of America.

To
Shana Marie Lewis
and
Edmund and Erma Rzepnicki

Contents

List of Tables and Figures

Figures

Tables

Acknowledgments

Implementation of the Illinois/West Virginia Project would have been impossible without the cooperation and assistance of a number of individuals. Foremost, we want to thank the child welfare workers who spent untold hours learning and applying new methods and completing endless research forms. Without their dedication, this work would not have been possible. We are indebted to The Catholic Charities of Chicago, especially Everett Petlicki, Kathy McGowan, Pat Griffith, and Balgrim Ragoonanan of the Foster Care Services Department, whose active involvement and enthusiasm were instrumental to the success of the field test in Illinois and to Director Gregory Coler of the Illinois Department of Children and Family Services. In West Virginia, we appreciate the contributions of administrative personnel from the Department of Welfare who assisted us by creating a hospitable environment for the research endeavor. Our thanks go to Margie Hale in the state office, Charles Young, Gay Gilbert, and Lucy Eates for their help in all aspects of the field test, including the continual encouragement of staff participation.

The contributions in time and energy of our research staff were invaluable. Project Coordinator Teresa Kilbane reviewed literature, designed instruments for data collection, and assisted with data analysis. Lea Cloninger and Andrew Stannard as Research Associates were responsible for data collection, coding, computer entry, and data cleaning. In addition to performing data collection and coding functions, Susan Young helped train workers in West Virginia and provided ongoing consultation at the test site in Fairmont, West Virginia. Special thanks are due to Mary Wolski who carried out numerous secretarial tasks essential to our efforts.

We wish to express our gratitude to Jane Hunsinger and Charles Gershenson of the United States Children's Bureau for their advice and guidance throughout the project.

Decision Making in
Child Welfare Services

1 INTRODUCTION

All countries confront the problem of providing for dependent, neglected, and abused children.[1] While the exact form of institutional response will differ in relation to a country's political and economic structure, its culture and its tradition, the same general kinds of child welfare services have been developed everywhere.[2]

Literature from the United States, Canada, and several Western European countries reflects a shared concern about children who reside in unplanned, substitute care arrangements and a growing recognition of the importance of making permanent plans for these children.[3] The American response to this problem took shape in the early 1970s when government at the local, state, and federal levels undertook to fund permanency planning projects.[4] Permanency planning projects were charged with developing and testing procedures that would increase the likelihood that children would move out of substitute care arrangements into permanent family homes either through restoration to their biological families, termination of parental rights and subsequent adoption, court appointment of a legal guardian, or planned emancipation for older children. Long-term foster care, if it was a planned outcome supported by the use of written agreements between foster parents and child care agencies, was recognized as an appropriate option for some children.

1

Permanency planning projects have had a direct effect on the substantive aspects of social work practice in child welfare. However, if change was to endure, it was recognized that reform would have to go beyond the implementation of new procedures for use by direct service staff. Advocacy groups pressed for a variety of policy and legal reforms including changes in federal policy and funding practices and in juvenile court procedures. The need for information systems to track a child's progress toward permanency goals, of regular review of all youngsters in out-of-home care, and of the importance of enacting new laws and modifying existing laws to facilitate adoption of children was recognized. The changes pursued resulted in significant modifications in the child welfare system over the past decade.[5]

Permanency planning projects were concerned with children already in placement. The question "What is the best permanent plan for children for whom out-of-home placement decisions had already been made?" was the point of departure for these research and demonstration efforts. The intake process and the critical decisions made during that process were not dealt with.

Reduction of placement through services to children in their own homes became the agenda for the 1980s. Meeting this agenda required the articulation of procedures for decision making at intake. Guidelines for making intake decisions would, when interfaced with the methods developed through permanency projects, provide guidance for child welfare staff in making all decisions from the point of initial contact through case termination. The development and testing of procedures for decision making at intake was a main objective of the project reported in this book.

Overview of the Book

In chapter 2, we briefly review the literature on the subject of decision making in child welfare and address a series of questions such as What support for decision making does the child welfare worker receive from professional standards of practice, the professional literature, statutory law, and agency policy? We shall argue that these sources provide little support and, in chapter 3, we will address the question "What are the strategies that workers employ in making difficult decisions and what costs accrue from the strategies used?" Implications for social work practice in child welfare of certain systemic reforms are reviewed in the last part of this chapter. The model that we developed to guide us in articulating a framework for decision making is described in chapter 4. Examples of the decision-making procedures tested during the project are presented.

The field test sites, research design, families served, and workers who participated in the project are described in chapter 5. In addition, the results of the reliability tests of our decision-making criteria are reported. In chapters 6 and 7, the results of the field test are presented. Usefulness of the experimental procedures was examined in relation to process variables such as the amount of time workers spent in decision-making activities (chapter 6); and in relation to decision outcomes, recidivism of cases, and worker satisfaction with the procedures (chapter 7). In the final chapter, we will explore the implications of our work for social work practice in child welfare, for administrators of agencies who must concern themselves with the implementation of practice innovations, and for social work education.

Notes and References

1. See, for example, Gunther Kaiser, "Child Abuse in West Germany," Victimology, Vol. 2, No. 2 (Summer 1977), pp. 294–306; H. Agathonos, N. Stathacopoulou, H. Adam, and S. Nakou, "Child Abuse, and Neglect in Greece: Sociomedical Aspects," Child Abuse and Neglect: The International Journal, Vol. 6, No. 3 (1982), pp. 307–311; F. M. Martin, K. Murray, and H. Millar, "The Role of 'Children's Hearings' in Child Abuse and Neglect," Child Abuse and Neglect: The International Journal, Ibid., pp. 313–320; L. Nathan and W. T. Hwang, "Child Abuse in an Urban Centre in Malaysia," Child Abuse and Neglect: The International Journal, Vol. 5, No. 3 (1981), pp. 241–248; A. Kahn and S. B. Kamerman, "Child Abuse: A Comparative Perspective," in Child Abuse: An Agenda for Action, eds. G. Gerbner, C. J. Ross, and E. Zigler (New York: Oxford University Press, 1980), pp. 118–132.

2. A. Kadushin, Child Welfare Services, 3d ed. (New York: Macmillan Publishing Co., Inc., 1980), p. 631.

3. S. E. Palmer, Children in Long-Term Care—Their Experiences and Progress (n.p.: Welfare Grants Directorate of the National Department of Health and Welfare, 2d ed., 1976); K. L. Levitt, "A Canadian Approach to Permanent Planning," Child Welfare, Vol. LX, No. 2 (February 1981), pp. 109–112; A. Kjonstad, "Child Abuse and Neglect: Viewed in Relation to 12 Fundamental Principles in a Western Social and Legal System," Child Abuse and Neglect: The International Journal, Vol. 5, No. 4 (1981), pp. 421–429; M. Adcock, "Planning Long-Term Care for the Abused Child," Child Abuse and Neglect: The International Journal, Vol. 3, No. 3/4 (1979), pp. 1005–1009; J. Triseliotis, "Introduction," in New Developments in Foster Care and Adoption, ed. J. Triseliotis (London: Routledge and Kegan Paul Ltd., 1980), p. 1; E. D. Gambrill, "Resources on Foster Care and Adoption in Britain," Children and Youth Services Review, Vol. 3, Nos. 1/2 (1981), pp. 77–83.

4. A. Emlen et al. Overcoming Barriers to Planning for Children in Foster Care, (Portland, Oregon: Regional Research Institute for Human Services, Portland State University, 1977); T. J. Stein, E. D. Gambrill, and K. T. Wiltse, Children in Foster Homes: Achieving Continuity of Care, (New York: Praeger Publishing Co., 1978).

5. These changes are discussed in detail at the end of chapter 2.

2 STUDIES OF DECISION MAKING IN CHILD WELFARE AND SOURCES OF INFORMATION FOR DECISION MAKING

Of all of the tasks performed by child welfare workers, decision making is perhaps the most critical. Decisions made regarding the exact nature of family problems, whether problems identified can be resolved while children remain in their own homes, or whether to recommend out-of-home care should have profound consequences for the families served.

The central role of decision making in child welfare practice has long been recognized here and abroad.[1] Practice has been studied extensively in an effort to ascertain the procedures that workers follow in making choices. The evidence shows that worker skill in decision making is not good. A main objective of this chapter is to consider some of the reasons why this is so. We begin with a brief review of the literature on the subject of decision making in child welfare. We will summarize the principal findings of a body of literature that has been extensively reviewed elsewhere and bring the reader up to date by reporting the results of the most recent investigations as they pertain to decision making at the time of intake. Next, several issues deemed salient to understanding the decision-making process such as information, decision-making criteria and rules, and the role of professional judgment in selecting options are discussed. This highlights some of the conditions that are necessary for reliable decision making. Subsequently, decision-making strategies are re-

5

viewed and the question "Why is the state-of-the-art regarding decision making in child welfare so poor?" is addressed. Finally, changes in the child welfare system that influenced us in developing decision-making procedures that were field tested in the Illinois/West Virginia project are reviewed.

Decision-Making Studies: A Brief Review

Three stages can be identified in the study of decision making in child welfare. The first we call the *exhortive stage,* the second, the *investigatory stage,* and the third, the *developmental phase,* which is reflected in the work of permanency planning projects.

The exhortive phase began in the late 1950s. Pursuant to the seminal work of Maas and Engler,[2] in which they documented the drift of children in long-term foster care, attention was drawn to the need for a decision-making framework to guide child welfare workers in making critical choices.[3] It was recommended that practice be studied in an effort to learn how practitioners make decisions. Presumably, a decision-making framework could be developed using knowledge gained in this manner.

Following these recommendations, investigators began to study the decision-making behavior of child welfare workers. How do practicing child welfare staff make decisions? was the question they addressed. The decisions of concern included whether to place children in out-of-home care,[4] where they should be placed,[5] and when they should be reunited with their birth parents.[6] Whether protective services should be offered to families[7] and what factors influence a child protective service workers' decisions to recommend court action in cases of child abuse involving physical injury are additional decision points studied.[8]

The findings from this body of work do not provide reason for optimism that child welfare workers are skilled decision makers. The principles of practice that investigators sought to uncover remain elusive. Some examples of what was learned will illustrate this point.

It is reasonable to assume that a worker's assessment of parental functioning and the availability of resources to assist parents whose functioning is minimal would exert a strong influence on the decision whether to place a child in foster care. Both Boehm[9] and Shinn[10] report that a worker's evaluation of maternal care plays such a role. Phillips, Shyne, Sherman, and Haring,[11] however, report that "neither the mother's functioning nor her relationship to the child were important considerations in reaching out-of-home placement decisions." Rather, they found that "traits of the father were the single most important cluster of variables" in two-parent families.

In contrast to this are findings from a study reported by Mech[12] in which factors related to placement could not be discerned, the work of Runyan and his colleagues who, likewise, were unable to describe the decision-making process that results in the placement of children in foster care,[13] and data reported by Ryan and Morris[14] and Stein,[15] both of whom inform us that diagnostic criteria do not play a role in decisions made at intake. Jenkins and Schroeder,[16] however, report that workers use a cornucopia of diagnostic aids during intake including the social investigation and information from psychological consultants as well as school, medical, and court records.

Data on the relationship between the availability of community resources and decisions made are also equivocal. Shyne,[17] Jenkins and Sauber,[18] and Thoburn[19] suggest that resource availability affects the decisions that are made (Shyne) and that placements could be avoided if resources such as day care and homemakers were available (Jenkins and Sauber). Thoburn, from her study in Britain, reports a discrepancy between the views of parents and those of caseworkers regarding the use of community resources and prevention of placement. Parents thought that "removal could have been avoided for about a third of the children, whereas social workers thought that it could have been avoided in only four cases."[20] Luce[21] reports that workers see children's needs in terms of services that are available. Gruber,[22] Stein,[23] and Rapp[24] found no association between the availability of resources and prevention of placement.

In order to learn about the factors that influence protective service workers to recommend court action, Craft and his colleagues[25] manipulated four factors in 16 cases presented to practicing protective service workers. These factors were (1) severity of injury, (2) explanations of how the injury was sustained (Were they consistent or inconsistent with the type and the location of the injury?) (3) the presence or absence of prior reports, and (4) parental conduct at the time of the report which was described as positive or negative.

Each of the 38 workers involved in this study reported his or her judgment regarding case disposition for all 16 cases. Workers tended to recommend court action for cases where a prior report existed, when the reaction of the parents was negative, and when the explanation of the injury was inconsistent with the type and/or extent of injury. "Seriousness of injury interacted with the remaining three variables under study such that the previous record of child abuse, the parental reaction, and the consistency of the explanation of the injury had greater impact when the injury was described as serious than when it was described as mild."[26] Others have reported that severity and chronicity are important factors in decisions to recommend services to families.[27] But, Craft and his colleagues report substantial disagreement among child protective service workers regarding the appropriateness of court action in a child abuse case. This disagreement is most evident when the injury is serious and where there is mix of negative and positive case characteristics.[28] Disagreement among workers is attributed to individual bias, which is seen as a major decision-making factor, rather than specific case characteristics.

The idea that a previous record of abuse increases the likelihood that court action will be recommended is contrary to Seaberg's[29] findings which were based on a secondary analysis of one data set from David Gil's national survey. Seaberg found that a prior record of abuse was inversely related to recommendations for court action.

Wolock, who studied the judgments of protective service workers about the severity of child abuse and neglect cases, informs us that judgments varied as a function of the severity of social and economic problems in the areas served by protective service staff. Specifically, workers in district offices with more severe caseloads judged vignettes provided by the author as less severe. Conversely, workers from offices with less severe caseloads judged the vignettes as more severe.[30]

As noted above, studies of decision making in child welfare proceeded on the assumption that practice principles to guide child welfare staff in making decisions existed, and that these principles were discoverable through investigations of practice. From the literature reviewed here and elsewhere,[31] it would appear that these assumptions were not correct. Now let us turn to the subject of information and to a consideration of some conditions that are necessary to facilitate reliable decision making.

Information

Decision making may be viewed as a three-stage process. First, information must be gathered using criteria which enable the practitioner to sort data into categories of relevant and irrelevant information. Rules are then applied which result in differential weighting of categories. Through this latter process, meaning is assigned to categories of information according to their relevance for making the decision of concern. For example, in cases where nonsupervision is alleged, parental behavior should be differentially weighted in relation to a child's age and self-help skills, and the availability of a client's personal resources as well as those that the agency can offer. In some instances, the application of rules is sufficient to reach a decision. The decision whether to provide services, and the type of service to provide, can be made readily if there is medical evidence that a child is malnourished and evidence that a parent lacks the knowledge, skills, and/or resources to obtain and prepare nutritionally balanced meals.

In cases where the evidence is not clear cut, professional judgment must be applied to reach a decision. Further information on the subject of professional judgment will be presented at a later time. Here, we will address the topics of decision-making criteria and decision-making rules.

Criteria and rules for decision making in child welfare may come from any one or a combination of the the following sources: (1) professional values and standards, (2) the professional literature, (3) statutory law, or (4) agency policy.

Professional Values and Standards for Decision Making

Acting in the best interests of children is a main concern in the United States and abroad.[32] In the American tradition, the best interest of the child standard has been used to guide practitioners through the process of gathering data as well as in the process of assigning meaning to information.

This standard expresses the value that societies place on children. As a long-range social objective, the desire to take actions that will further the physical and emotional well-being of children is laudable. As a guide for decision making, however, the best interest standard has three major deficiencies.

First, once we move beyond minimum standards in areas such as a child's physical, educational, and emotional well-being, there is neither social nor professional consensus as to what is in the best interest of all children. Even at the lower end of the child care spectrum people are likely to disagree about the conditions that are necessary to ensure optimal child development.[33] The further away we move from minimum conditions, the greater the disagreement is apt to be. This poses a dilemma for the individual social worker whose values or biases are interjected into the decision-making process under the guise of applying scientific principles.[34]

Our inability to make the long-range predictions called for in the use of the best interest standard is a further limitation to its use.[35] Data from a number of sources, including longitudinal investigations of child development and thorough reviews of child development research, force the conclusion that the state of knowledge is limited with regard to making the predictions of primary concern to decision makers using the best interest of the child standard.[36]

Finally, decision making, particularly in the early phases of intervention, should be guided by concern for the family unit. Any decision-making rule that emphasizes the rights of children or of parents creates an artificial dichotomy for the decision maker, whose main task it is to maintain the family unit. Giving primacy to one party over another detracts from the importance of balancing the right of parents to raise their children free from outside intervention against the right of children to be protected from undue harm.

The British experience is instructive here. Prior to passage of the 1975 Children Act, parental rights were of prime importance. Social workers were accused of reunifying families regardless of risk to children. The balance was shifted in 1975 to the rights of children. Now the concern is that parental ties will be quickly severed in order to free children for adoption.[37] Decision making in child welfare is difficult as it is. The polarization created by emphasizing the rights of only one party compounds an already difficult situation.

The Professional Literature   The best interest standard must be viewed as an open-ended invitation to gather information on all facets of family life. The breadth implied by use of this standard is reinforced in the professional literature, which directs the practitioner to gather information in a variety of areas descriptive of a client's life but offers little guidance for using information to make decisions.

Workers are asked to describe clients on quantifiable dimensions, including health status, income, number of marriages, length of time at current job and at present place of residence, and to draw inferences from observations regarding a client's degree of independence, dependence, parents' level of concern for their children, whether families are close-knit, cooperative, fastidious, appear to be emotionally disturbed, and so forth.[38] Add to this the current emphasis on a client's ecology and the number of areas in which information could be gathered expands dramatically.

The data base for making decisions goes well beyond the information that is gathered by the child welfare worker. Jenkins and Schroeder[39] inform us that, in addition to the information that is recorded during the social investigation (which is used 88 percent of the time for decision making at intake) information from "psychological tests, psychiatric examinations, school records, health records or examinations, court reports, case information from other agencies [and information from] other [sources] may play a role in intake decision making."

Statutory Law is ambiguous regarding the conditions that constitute abuse and neglect, and offers little guidance to child welfare workers or juvenile court judges in making critical decisions.[40]

Except for extreme situations where the child's condition, the location of an injury, and the child's age interact so as to eliminate any doubt that abuse has been perpetrated, professionals agree that it is very difficult to determine what is and what is not child maltreatment.[41]

Agency Policy should provide guidance for staff in making critical decisions. Agencies have been faulted for either failing to formulate policy or for setting policies that are so vague regarding agency philosophy and goals as to provide little in the way of guidance for their staff.[42]

There is reason to believe that this situation is changing. Recognition of the importance of operationalizing policy to guide staff in making decisions and efforts to conform local policy to the federal requirements in the Adoption Assistance and Child Welfare Act of 1980 are sources for change.[43]

Discussion

The sources to which a worker might turn for guidance in making decisions —professional standards, the professional literature, statutory law, and agency policy—offer little in the way of assistance with direct application to decision making in practice situations.

Given the shortcomings just reviewed, the finding that child welfare workers gather excessive amounts of information, the use of which for decision making is not clear, should not come as a surprise.[44] The sheer volume of information workers use will pose problems for the decision maker given the limited information-processing capacity of the human mind.[45] Equally troublesome is the evidence that a decision maker's confidence increases as the amount of information available increases, even though there is no corresponding increase in predictive accuracy.[46]

In lieu of guidance from the four sources from which criteria could be culled, the practitioner has little choice but to exercise a large measure of individual discretion in deciding what information to gather and what meaning to assign to available data. That workers exercise a great deal of personal discretion and the fact that personal values and idiosyncratic judgments exert a strong influence on decision making has been a consistent finding from studies of decision making in child welfare as well as from reports of judicial decision making.[47]

Since individual discretion plays a large a role in decision making, the poor inter-judge reliability reported from studies of decision making is not surprising. For example, Phillips et al.[48] compared intake decisions of social workers from three agencies with those of independent judges, each of whom had more than five years of experience in child welfare. "The judges agreed with each other and with the workers on less than one-half of the cases; when they did agree, they did not identify the same factors."[49] Likewise, Wolins[50] found that agreement between worker–judges, basing their decisions on material in the case record, was poor (chi-square = .47). But reliability increased to .81 when they received only the information considered most salient to the decision. Further confirmation of the lack of criteria is provided by Golan[51] from her study of workers in community mental health centers, where she found a "lack of uniformity in data gathered." Superfluous information was gathered and information that seemed essential to intake decisions was missing. She attributed her findings to the lack of guidance about what information was most important to obtain.[52]

Notes and References

1. "Child Welfare as a Field of Social Work Practice," (Position paper of the Child Welfare League of America and the U.S. Children's Bureau, New York, Child Welfare League of America, 1959), pp. 19–20; Martin Wolins, "A Proposed Research Program for the Child Welfare League of America" (New York: Child Welfare League of America, 1959), pp. 13–14; David Fanshel, "Research in Child Welfare: A Critical Analysis," XLI, No. 10 (1962), pp. 484–507; Kermit T. Wiltse, "Current Issues and New Directions in Foster Care," in *Child Welfare Strategies in the Coming Years* (Washington, D.C.: U.S. Dept. of Health, Education and Welfare, DHEW Publication Number (OHDS) 78-30158, 1978), pp. 51–89; Margaret Adcock, "Dilemmas in Planning Long-Term Care," in *New Developments in Foster Care and Adoption* ed. John Triseliotis (London: Routledge and Kegan Paul, Ltd., 1980), Ch. 1; June Thoburn, *Captive Clients: Social Work with Families of Children Home on Trial* (London: Routledge and Kegan Paul, Ltd., 1980), ch. 7.

2. Henry Maas and Richard Engler, *Children in Need of Parents* (New York: Columbia University Press, 1959).

3. Wolins, op cit.; Fanshel, op cit.; Edmund V. Mech, "Decision Analysis in Foster Care Practice," in *Foster Care in Question* ed. Helen D. Stone (New York: Child Welfare League of America, 1970), pp. 26–51; Donald Brieland, Kenneth Watson, Philip Hovda, David Fanshel, and John J. Carey, *Differential Use of Manpower: A Team Model for Foster Care* (New York: Child Welfare League of America, 1968), p. 8.

4. Sally E. Palmer, "The Decision to Separate Children From Their Natural Parents," *Social Work,* Vol. 39 (1971), pp. 82–87; Bernice Boehm, "An Assessment of Family Adequacy in Protective Cases," *Child Welfare,* Vol. 41 (January 1962), pp. 10–16; Bernice Boehm, "Protective Services for Neglected Children," *Social Work Practice: Proceedings of the National Conference on Social Welfare* (New York: Columbia University Press, 1967), pp. 109–125; Michael H. Phillips, Ann W. Shyne, Edmund A. Sherman, and Barbara L. Haring, *Factors Associated with Placement Decisions in Child Welfare* (New York: Child Welfare League of America, 1971); Eugene B. Shinn, "Is Placement Necessary? An Experimental Study of Agreement Among Caseworkers in Making Foster Care Decisions" (diss., Columbia University, 1969); State of New York, Child Welfare Reform Act of 1979, Laws of 1979, Chapters 610 and 611 (May 31, 1979). Thoborn, op cit.; Margaret A. Lynch and Jacqueline Roberts, *Consequences of Child Abuse* (London: Academic Press, Inc., 1982).

5. Scott Briar, "Clinical Judgment in Foster Care Placement," *Child Welfare,* Vol. 42 (1963), pp. 161–169.

6. Mary Ann Jones, Renee Neuman, and Ann W. Shyne, *A Second Chance for Families: Evaluation of a Program to Reduce Foster Care* (New York: Child Welfare League of America, 1976); Arthur Emlen et al. *Overcoming Barriers to Planning for Children in Foster Care* (Portland, Oregon: Regional Research Institute for Human Services, Portland State University, 1977); Theodore J. Stein, Eileen D. Gambrill and Kermit T. Wiltse, *Children in Foster Homes: Achieving*

Continuity in Care (New York: Praeger Publishers, division of Holt, Rinehart & Winston, 1978). See Thorpe (1974) and Aldgate (1978) cited in Thoburn, op cit., p. 7.

7. Joan Di Leonardi, "Decision Making in Protective Services," *Social Welfare,* 59 (June, 1980), pp. 356–364; F. M. Martin, Kathleen Murray, and Helen Millar, "The Role of 'Children's Hearings' in Child Abuse and Neglect," *Child Abuse and Neglect: The International Journal,* Vol. 6 No. 3 (1982), pp. 313–320.

8. John L. Craft, Stephen W. Epley, and Cheryl D. Clarkson, "Factors Influencing Legal Dispositions in Child Abuse Investigations," *Journal of Social Service Research,* Vol. 4, No. 1 (Fall, 1980), pp. 31–46; James R. Seaberg, "Disposition in Physical Child Abuse," *California Psychologist,* Vol. 1, No. 1 (1978), pp. 3–11.

9. Boehm, *An Assessment of Family Adequacy,* op cit.

10. Shinn, op cit.

11. Phillips et al., op cit.

12. See Mech, op cit., p. 44.

13. Desmond K. Runyan et al., "Determinants of Foster Care Placement for the Maltreated Child," *Child Abuse and Neglect: The International Journal,* Vol. 6, No. 3 (1982), pp. 343–350.

14. William Ryan, and Laura B. Morris, *Child Welfare Problems and Potentials* (Boston, Mass.: Massachusetts Committee on Children and Youth, 1967).

15. Theodore J. Stein, "A Content Analysis of Social Caseworker and Client Interaction in Foster Care," D.S.W. diss., Berkeley, California: School of Social Welfare, 1974.

16. Shirley Jenkins and Anita G. Schroeder, *Intake: The Discriminant Function—A Report on the National Study on Social Services Intake for Children and Their Families* Prepared by Westat Inc, for the U.S. Dept. of Health, Education and Welfare (Rockville, Maryland: September 1979).

17. Ann W. Shyne, *The Need for Foster Care* (New York: Child Welfare League of America, 1969).

18. Shirley Jenkins, and Mignon Sauber, *Paths to Child Placement: Family Situations Prior to Foster Care* (New York: The Community Council of Greater New York, 1966).

19. Thoburn, op cit.

20. Ibid., p. 131.

21. Dean Luce, *Child Placement Decisions* (Urbana, Illinois: University of Illinois, School of Social Work, 1975).

22. Alan R. Gruber, *Children in Foster Care: Destitute, Neglected. . . . Betrayed* (New York: Human Sciences Press, 1978).

23. Stein, A Content Analysis, op cit.

24. Charles A. Rapp, "Effect of the Availability of Family Support Services on Decisions about Child Placement," *Social Work* Research & Abstracts, Vol. 18, No. 1 [Spring 1982], pp. 21–27.

25. Craft et al., op cit, p. 35.

26. Ibid., p. 42.

27. di Leonardi, op cit.; Helen Rosen, cited in Isabel Wolock, "Community Characteristics and Staff Judgments in Child Abuse and Neglect Cases," *Social Work Research and Abstracts,* Vol. 18, No. 2 (Summer 1982), pp. 9–15.

28. Craft et al., op cit., p. 42.

29. Seaberg, op cit.

30. Isabel Wolock, "Community Characteristics and Staff Judgments in Child Abuse and Neglect Cases," *Social Work Research and Abstracts,* Vol. 18, No. 2 (Summer 1982), pp. 9–15.

31. For a detailed review of this research see Stein, Gambrill, and Wiltse, op cit.

32. R. Walton, "The Best Interests of the Child," *British Journal of Social Work,* Vol. 6, No.

3 (1976), pp. 307–313; Asbjorn Kjonstad, "Child Abuse and Neglect: Viewed in Relation to 12 Fundamental Principles in a Western Social and Legal System," *Child Abuse and Neglect: The International Journal,* Vol. 5, No. 4 (1981), pp. 421–429.

33. Parents have successfully challenged state laws regarding compulsory school attendance as well as required medical care. See Robert H. Mnookin, *Child, Family and State—Problems and Materials on Children and the Law* (Boston, Mass.: Little, Brown and Company, 1978), pp. 43–57, 68–76.

34. Emlen et al., op cit.; Craft et al., p. 42; June Thoburn, "Good Enough Care? A Study of Children Who Went Home 'On Trial'," *Child Abuse and Neglect: The International Journal,* Vol. 3, No. 1 (1979), p. 77.

35. The best interest test could be construed to focus the decision maker's attention on formulating short-term predictions based on current knowledge. However, in its current construction, attention is directed to making long-range predictions.

36. Arlene Skolnick, *The Intimate Environment: Exploring Marriage and the Family,* 2d ed. (Boston, Mass.: Little, Brown and Company, 1978), p. 354; Sheldon H. White et al., *Federal Programs for Young Children; Review and Recommendations: Volume I: Goals and Standards of Public Programs for Children* (Washington, D.C.: Superintendent of Documents, 1973), p. 130; Joseph Goldstein, Anna Freud, and Albert J. Solnit, *Beyond the Best Interests of the Child* (New York: The Free Press, 1973), p. 6; Kjonstad, op cit., p. 422.

37. Rosamund, Thorpe, "The Experiences of Children and Parents Living Apart: Implications and Guidelines for Practice," in John Triseliotis, op cit., p. 85.

38. Rita Dukette, *Structured Assessment: A Decision-making Guide for Child Welfare* (Chicago, Illinois: U.S. Dept. of Health, Education and Welfare: Region V, April 1978); Michael H. Phillips, Barbara L. Harin, and Ann W. Shyne, *A Model for Intake Decisions in Child Welfare* (New York: Child Welfare League of America, 1972).

39. Jenkins and Schroeder, op cit., p. 19.

40. The argument that the law must be broad to give judges sufficient discretion in making case-by-case decisions is not persuasive. See Stanford N. Katz, *When Parents Fail: The Law's Response to Family Breakdown* (Boston, Mass.: Beacon Press, 1971), p. 62–63. As Wald points out, judges "lack training relevant to making decisions regarding intervention and appropriate dispositions. Few juvenile court judges are trained in psychology or other behavioral sciences" (p. 8). He goes on to note that most of the social workers assigned to court are not sufficiently trained to provide guidance in making the decisions of concern. (See Michael S. Wald, "State Intervention on Behalf of Endangered Children—A Proposed Legal Response," *Child Abuse and Neglect: The International Journal,* Vol. 6, No. 1 (1982), pp. 3–46.)

41. Saad Z. Nagi, *Child Maltreatment in the United States: A Challenge to Social Institutions* (New York: Columbia University Press, p. 15); Jill E. Korbin (ed.), *Child Abuse and Neglect: Cross-Cultural Perspectives* (Berkeley, California: University of California Press, 1981).

42. Stein, Gambrill, and Wiltse, op cit., p. 17.

43. United States Senate, Committe on Finance, *Adoption Assistance and Child Welfare Act of 1980,* 96th Congress, 2d Session (Washington, D.C.: U.S. Government Printing Office, June 17, 1980).

44. Stein, "A Content Analysis," op cit.; Martin Wolins, *Selecting Foster Parents* (New York: Columbia University Press, 1963); Naomi Golan, "How Caseworkers Decide: A Study of the Association of Selected Applicant Factors With Worker Decision in Admission Services," *Social Service Review,* Vol. 43 (1969), pp. 289–296; Donald Brieland, *An Experimental Study in the Selection of Adoptive Parents at Intake* (New York: Child Welfare League of America, 1959).

45. Robin M. Hogarth, *Judgment and Choice: The Psychology of Decision* (New York: John Wiley and Sons, 1980, p. 4); It has been estimated that the number of categories of information

that a person can process in immediate memory is no more than seven, plus or minus two. See Irving L. Janis and Leon Mann, *Decision Making: A Psychological Analysis of Conflict, Choice, and Commitment* (New York: The Free Press, 1977), p. 22.

46. Hogarth, op cit., p. 31.
47. See Stein, Gambrill, and Wiltse, p. 20.
48. Phillips et al., *Factors Associated with Placement Decisions,* op cit.
49. Ibid., p. 84.
50. Wolins, op cit., pp. 72–73.
51. Golan, op cit., pp. 289–296.
52. Ibid., p. 11.

3 JUDGMENT AND DECISION MAKING

Earlier we said that the use of professional judgment will influence the decision-making process when the application of decision-making rules does not point to a correct alternative. When the evidence is not clear-cut, the exercise of judgment can be critical in selecting a final option.

In reality, professional judgment may be influential at all stages of the decision-making process. If there are no guidelines to give direction to data-gathering tasks nor rules for using information, the role of judgment can be expected to influence the process throughout. Progression through all points in a decision chain, beginning with the determination of what information is most relevant through a final decision regarding what action to take, will be guided by the discretion of the individual worker. Given the presence of rules that direct the decision maker to items of information that are most germane to the decision and that provide direction for using information, judgment will still play a role in making a final decision in cases where the evidence leads to ambiguous conclusions.

Professionals, whether social workers, psychologists, or psychiatrists, are expected to have special expertise in forming judgments. Such expertise is part of a claim to professional status. Whether this claim is justified is a legitimate question. The evidence reviewed thus far could lead easily to the conclusion

17

that professional judgment is an elegant label applied to behavior which, when observed in lay people, would be called simple bias. As Austin states, "Limited empirical evidence indicates that professional judgment is too often inaccurate and inconsistent and may not reflect a client's actual situation."[1]

It is often noted that direct service staff in public agencies are not likely to hold a master's of social work degree. Without graduate training, it is questionable whether the behavior of staff can be classified as professional. At present, only a minority of direct service workers hold the MSW degree. From data reported in 1978 by Shyne and Schroeder collected for a national survey of public agencies in 41 states, we learn that "only 25 percent of the children were assigned to workers with social work degrees, usually bachelor's degrees," which accounted for 16 percent of the sample. Thus, only 9 percent of the casework staff in the agencies studied held an advanced social work degree.[2]

Yet, social workers with master's degrees were involved in many of the studies of decision making to which we have referred. Briar, Shinn, Jones et al., Stein, and Stein, Gambrill, and Wiltse[3] report that between 59 percent (Jones) and 100 percent (Stein) of the workers in their studies held an MSW degree. Also, the judges who participated in the study conducted by Phillips et al.,[4] whose reliability in decision making was tested, were selected specifically because they had more than five years of experience in child welfare. And, if the literature is correct in suggesting that a majority of professionally trained social workers become supervisors in public agency settings, and bearing in mind the importance of the supervisor's educational and consultive roles,[5] it is quite reasonable to suggest that the decision-making behavior of staff, regardless of the degrees they hold, will be influenced by social work graduate education.

It is questionable whether graduate social work education equips staff to make the kinds of decisions they confront in practice in child welfare agencies. The limited evidence available suggests that it does not.[6] What, then, are the tactics that workers employ to make decisions? In an effort to cast some light on this question, we will turn to the psychological literature and to a review of *judgmental strategies* that research has shown to influence the decision-making behavior of individuals.

Knowledge Structures and Judgmental Strategies

Through a combination of learning experiences, practitioners develop a knowledge base which includes theories, beliefs, propositions, and schemas[7] as well as a set of expectations about the world which they use to lend order to what would otherwise be a chaotic physical reality. The decision maker must gain access to these knowledge structures. Whether the stimuli in any situation fit with one's theories, beliefs, and expectations and, if so, in what way, must be determined.

Judgmental strategies that are used to gain access to knowledge structures are reviewed next. Space limitations preclude an extensive review of all of the research that is pertinent to this subject.

Judgmental Strategies

Kahneman and Tversky[8] conducted a series of experiments to learn how people judge the likely outcome of uncertain events. They identified two heuristics that guide the judgmental process. These are the *representative heuristic* and the *availability heuristic.* Nisbett and Ross add to this a third intuitive strategy that people employ whereby they assign weights to data according to the presumed relevance of the data for furthering understanding of a situation.[9]

The Representative Heuristic is used to facilitate assignment of information to categories. Assignment is said to proceed on the basis of similarities between the object to be assigned and one's cognitive representations about members of different categories.[10] This allows the decision maker to "reduce many inferential tasks to what are essentially simple similarity judgments."[11]

The following vignette, which is similar to those used by Kahneman and Tversky in their experiments, will illustrate the operation of the representative heuristic.

> Emily Cartwright, a 25-year-old black woman is the single parent of three children, age 7, 9, and 10. Mrs. Cartwright and her children live in a three-room apartment in one of the poorest sections of the city. Having paid her rent and purchased groceries, Mrs. Cartwright has little, if any, money left for luxuries. The children receive no allowance. Mrs. Cartwright often complains of the difficulties involved in raising three children without the help of another adult. As for herself, her social contacts are limited to interaction with neighbors. She cannot afford a babysitter and is rarely, if ever, able to afford even the cost of a movie ticket. Is it likely that Mrs. Cartwright's children: (1) are recipients of an AFDC grant or (2) that Mrs. Cartwright works for a living?

The reader who selected option *1* is responding to the representative heuristic by making a judgment on the basis of several dominant characteristics of Mrs. Cartwright's situation. In fact, the correct guess would be option *2* for the simple reason that statistically the chances are far greater that Mrs. Cartwright will be employed than that she will be an AFDC mother.

Judgmental errors result from a failure to use base-rate information when a personality sketch is provided.[12] As regards the previous example, two points can be made on the subject of base rates. First, 72 percent of single mothers with children 6 to 17 years of age are in the labor force.[13] Secondly, AFDC recipients are counted as individuals, the majority of whom are children. There is no way to translate the number of recipients into the number of family units.[14] Without knowledge of how recipients are counted, such a translation may be attempted—which results in greatly overestimating the number of families on AFDC. Research shows that people do consider probabilities when case-specific data is not provided.[15] Thus, the question "What is the likelihood that a single-parent, female-headed family is receiving AFDC versus the likelihood that the mother is employed?" is apt to elicit a correct answer because case characteristics are not given. The brief sketch provided above may be descriptive of many poor families regardless of their source of income. Information which would permit a distinction between a working poor and an AFDC family is not provided.

The relevance of this example to the subject of decision making is that many professional judgments are made on the basis of limited information. This does not contradict the reports that workers gather excessive amounts of data, the use of which for decision making is not clear. Rather, it highlights the finding that decisions are often made based on information gained in early encounters with clients and that additional data does not alter a decision once it is made. For instance, Brieland, from his study of how adoptive applicants are selected, informs us that decisions are based on the information from the first half of the interview and that information collected during the second half bears no relation to the final decision.[16]

People often select an outcome that is representative of the input.[17] If information descriptive of a client fits a stereotype, the probabilities are that the prediction made will fit expectations of the stereotype regardless of the presence of factors that might limit the likelihood that the person is a member of the class. The fact that much of the knowledge base against which clients are compared comes from clinical studies rather than from controlled experimental investigations increases the chances that child welfare workers will make judgmental errors of this sort.

"Data that is gathered from people who come to the attention of professional therapists cannot be presumed to reflect the experiences of the population-at-large or of the population of persons with a given problem because the individuals interviewed have asked for help or been referred for it. Thus, they may differ in significant ways from others who have similar problems but do not receive assistance."[18] In addition, the theories that guide much clinical practice focus attention on personality disorders, with little attention to positive traits, and on the individual, with little attention to environmental variables.

The suggestion that confidence in judgment increases when input variables are redundant[19] compounds the problems that are created by stereotyping. Once a judgment has been made, subsequent input variables are apt to be selected on the basis of early classifications—e.g., we look for what we expect to see. Confidence may increase through a process of selecting input variables which confirm initial hypotheses, not by case-specific data.

Use of the representative heuristic is functional in our daily lives. Decisions whether to cross the street when we see a stranger walking toward us from the opposite direction or whether to purchase an automobile from a particular salesperson may depend partly on whether the person fits the perceptual category of safe or unsafe, trustworthy or untrustworthy.

Use of this heuristic creates a problem when it is the only judgmental strategy employed, even though, by itself, it cannot provide an adequate judgment.[20] In reality, whether to cross the street at the sight of an approaching stranger will depend, in part, upon the time of day, whether others are present in the environment, and one's judgment of the likelihood that others would respond to a call for help. When used alone, the representative heuristic will create problems if the known features of an object cannot categorize it definitively.[21] Once we have assigned a person to a category, our field of vision will narrow and categorical expectations may govern future observations. "The relative frequency of the categories in the population under consideration become the normatively appropriate guide to categorization to the extent that the known features of the object are ambiguous guides to categorization."[22]

The Availability Heuristic   Many of the judgments made by child welfare staff involve estimates of frequency, probability, and causality. The decision whether to open a case subsequent to a report of nonsupervision may depend on one's best judgment as to how often the child is likely to be left alone and the risk to the child if he or she is not supervised. The presumed causes of parental behavior will affect decisions regarding what services to offer.

It is rare that practitioners have exact answers to the questions of greatest concern. The frequency with which a child is left alone is very difficult to determine without continual surveillance of a family. Whether or not a child who is left alone will use self-help skills and whether or not a child will be injured cannot be wholly predicted.

Judgments of whether an event is frequent or probable and hypotheses regarding causality will be affected by evidence that is available in memory. Availability can be affected by the drama of an event, not solely by factors such as frequency and probability.[23] Slovic et al.[24] report that people "greatly overestimate the frequency and risk of death from dramatic, sensational causes such as accidents, homicides, cancer, botulism, and tornadoes. Underestimates are made when the cause is unspectacular . . . and common [such as] diabetes, stroke, tuberculosis, asthma, and emphysema."

Ease of recall contributes to judgments of events as probable, thus, availability of an event in memory is an appropriate cue. But, dramatic and sensational events are more readily accessible than are common and mundane happenings.

Several aspects of social work education and practice increase the chances that information available in memory will be disproportionately negative. Pathology, rather than health, is stressed in many of the theories that guide social work education. Thus, students may develop a *search set* that places heavy emphasis on selection of evidence to reinforce a pathological view of client behavior.

Because so much of our data regarding client characteristics come from clinical studies, incorrect associations may be formed and reinforced. The suggestion that parents who abuse their children are mentally ill is an example of what has been called an *illusory correlation effect.*[25] Despite the data showing that less than ten percent of all abusing parents are seriously mentally ill and the frequent suggestion that abusing parents do not appear to be different from a random sample of people selected from a downtown street, the "mental illness as cause" hypothesis persists.[26] Such hypotheses, once formed, are very difficult to change.

It is rare to find an intake schedule or checklist of client behaviors that draws attention to family strengths.[27] Based on our experiences, we would guess that the information recorded in most social investigations is overly negative in content. Moreover, we think it unlikely that workers receive follow-up information on cases that are closed save for those instances when abuse or neglect recur. If this is correct, most of the feedback available to staff about decisions made is negative. And, as Nisbett and Ross point out, "media may overexpose us to some events and underexpose us to others, ensuring that our later ease of recalling or imagining events will produce distorted estimates."[28] Since the vividness of information influences recall[29] and since the media attends to the most unsavory child abuse cases, there is yet another source from which negative information is added to the worker's recollections. The likelihood of seeing a family who is reported to protective services as mentally ill, abusive, or neglectful may be far greater than the chances of seeing the family as healthy, regardless of case-specific characteristics.

On the subject of feedback, Hogarth takes the position that the consequences of less-than-perfect judgments may not be as serious as Nisbett and Ross suggest.[30] According to Hogarth, the feedback that we receive regarding events may be used to modify judgments. He argues for a distinction between judgment and choice where the former may be seen as a series of links in a chain, each subject to modification based on later input, and with choice, the end product of the chain governed by judgment and subsequent modifications. There is little doubt that we process information in a sequential manner.[31] Adjustments in our field of vision can be made on the basis of new data. The critical question is "Are final judgments more likely to be influenced by early information or by the more recent information obtained?". The evidence is overwhelming that *primacy effects*[32] are a major determinant of the information-processing sequence.

> Primacy effects in information processing are the rule because people are theorists in their approach to information about the social and physical world. Early encountered information serves as the raw material for inferences about what the object is like. These inferences or theories about the nature of the object, in turn, bias the interpretation of later encountered information . . . theories about the nature of objects are revised insufficiently in response to discrepancies in the later presented information.[33]

Once judgments are made, they are amazingly intractable in the face of new evidence. Smith and Hocking, in discussing biases which are formed on the basis of how presenting problems are formulated, state:

> The initial formulation by professional workers of the family's problem is an important indicator of how a case will be handled. When this is based on an insufficiently comprehensive examination of all the relevant circumstances it is likely that relevant information arising subsequently is disregarded or not given proper importance; thus it seemed that bias became more and more pronounced through time. One example of this was a case where the initial formulation attached high importance to the psychiatric condition of the mother with little weight being attached to the child's total needs and safety. When the mother's mental condition subsequently improved, insufficient attention was paid to reassessing the situation with respect to the child's needs and the child later died as a result of nonaccidental injury.[34]

A further example is provided by Ross[35] in whose study people were assigned the task of distinguishing between real and fake suicide notes. Arbitrary ratings of successful, failed, or average were assigned to subjects on task performance. Subjects were later told that the feedback provided them was false. They were shown the experimenter's sheet on which they were assigned to success, failure, or average performance conditions. When later asked to estimate how well they had done on the original task and to predict how they would do on the same task in the future, their response suggested that the post experiment debriefing had never occurred. Subject judgments of themselves corresponded closely to the false ratings they had been assigned.

Since events are interpreted according to our perceptions and assuming that we are correct in suggesting that the perceptions held by child welfare workers are primarily negative, it is reasonable to expect that practitioners will make type II errors by predicting pathology where none exists.

We have said that the vividness of information influences recall where the more vivid the information the more accessible it is in memory. Vividness of information also influences the weighting of data. The more vivid the information, the greater is the weight assigned to it in making decisions. Thus, without clear rules for using information to select options, the biases that influence recall will also influence the final choice selected.

Causal Analysis   Unlike social scientists, whose concern is with classes of events, practitioners normally are concerned with characterizing the individual case as accurately as possible. That purpose is best served by allowing valid preconceptions and theories to influence one's characterizations, especially when the data are ambiguous.

There are three broad sets of circumstances in which the practice of allowing preconceptions to influence the characterization of data is normatively questionable. These are: (1) when the theory is held on poor grounds, e.g., if justification for applying the theory to the situation is not adequate; (2) when the theory is applied unconsciously in the belief that the data are being interpreted without the aid of theory (for example, when stereotypes of racial groups guide decisions about the behavior of individuals but the interpreter of the data insists that impressions are guided by factual observations not preconceived notions); and (3) when the theory preempts examination of the data, e.g., initial biases prevent the data-gatherer from observing the particulars of the case.[36]

It is likely that theories of causation come into play in the earliest stages of working with clients, influencing data that are gathered and decisions that are made. The worker who approaches assessment with the conviction that intrapsychic factors or environmental factors, by themselves, cause clients to behave in certain ways is prone to collecting data and to making decisions regarding intervention on the basis of his or her original theory of causation. Thus, the correctness of theories held and the willingness to modify them in the face of contradictory evidence are viewed as critical elements of decision making.

Use of the Representative Heuristic in Causal Analysis   A major fallacy in causal reasoning is that the cause of phenomenon must resemble the phenomenon. Thus, the suggestion that having been abused as a child causes the adult to abuse his own child has intuitive appeal since the cause resembles the effect.

And, it is assumed that significant events should have significant causes. To suggest that child abuse may have been an isolated incident caused by stress during a family crisis may seem less intuitively plausible than does an explanation that focuses on deep-seated pathology.

The fallacy we are referring to is evident in psychoanalytic thought and the circularity of many of the causal explanations that are offered. Behavior labeled as obsessive-compulsive, for example, is said to be caused by an obsessive-compulsive complex. A death instinct is posited to explain the behavior of soldiers during wartime.[37]

Reasoning of this sort is fairly common. "Political radicalism and nonconformity are attributed to the permissiveness in child-rearing practiced by generations of parents tutored by Dr. Spock; sex crimes are attributed to the accessibility of pornography to youths; and adult maladjustment is attributed to childhood trauma. By the same token, faithful pursuit of a paper route is deemed an early indicator of adult responsibility and entrepreneurial ambition. Such causal views do not conflict with well-established scientific laws of causality in the way that old wives' tales and superstitions do. Indeed, many such views may contain more than a germ of truth. But, it is hard to avoid the suspicion that the resemblance criterion is an important part of their appeal.[38]

This line of reasoning is particularly problematic when beliefs are held despite contradictory evidence. For example, despite the evidence of our inability to make long-range predictions of child development based solely on knowledge of parent–child interaction, professionals often act as though accurate predictions can be made. On this point, Nisbett and Ross, summarizing the work of Ross and Lepper and their colleagues, point out that: (1) When people already have a theory, before encountering any genuinely probative evidence, exposure to such evidence (whether it supports the theory, opposes the theory, or is mixed) will tend to result in more belief in the correctness of the original theory than normative dictates allow. (2) When people approach a set of evidence without a theory and then form a theory based on initial evidence, the theory will be resistant to subsequent evidence. (3) When people formulate a theory based on some putatively probative evidence and later discover that the evidence is false, the theory often survives such total discrediting.[39]

Trait versus Situational Explanations of Behavior   One of the more complex tasks confronting child welfare staff is the search for antecedents of problematic behavior. The question "What caused a caretaker to abuse or neglect a child?" begs for an answer. Decisions whether the presumed antecedents are to be found in the situational or environmental arenas or in the psychological makeup of the client, or both, will have serious implications for clients. There is a tendency in the mental health professions—one that is strongly reinforced in the literature—to attribute behavior to constant traits and dispositions of the actor, ignoring the effects of situational variables.

Use of the representative and the availability heuristic increases the chances that errors of this sort will be made. Our conceptual and linguistic organization of the world rely more on the ordering of people than they do on the ordering of situations.[40] Since we observe people acting, assumptions that a disposition of the actor, rather than situational factors, is causal, are easily drawn. In other words, actions of the actor are more readily seen as representative causes than are situational factors. And, traits and dispositions are readily available explanations of actions. Interestingly, however, "for a wide variety of behaviors and across a wide variety of situations, actors have been found to attribute their behavior relatively more to situational factors and observers, relatively more to dispositions of the actor."[41]

In general, the evidence suggests that predictions of behavior which are based on traits of the individual, as measured by paper and pencil tests or by observations of behavior in single situations, are low, rarely exceeding .30 for the former and .20 for the latter.[42] Without question, there are subsets of individuals whose behavior is consistent across situations.[43] There is research showing that correlation coefficients for traits such as friendliness and conscientiousness increase to .50 or .60 if the subset of individuals to whom the trait applies are first identified. In other words, rather than assuming that all people show consistency across situations, we must recognize that assumptions regarding constant traits apply to only a subsample of the population. Identifying this subsample is a necessary first step in making predictions based on assumptions regarding consistencies in behavior. Absent such evidence, we are on safer grounds in observing individuals in different situations and using evidence from such observations as a basis for predicting behavior.

The fact that clients are generally seen in a limited range of situations, always in a worker's office or in the client's home on a regular schedule, enacting a finite number of roles, reinforces assumptions regarding consistency of behavior and argues for gathering of assessment data using multiple methods in varying situations. However, this is no guarantee that information gathered will be accurate. It is still possible that observed discrepancies in behavior will be dismissed as irrelevant—as inconsequential variants on a norm—if our causal explanations are not subject to modification. As we pointed out above, perseverance of belief is very strong. People do have a tendency to pick and choose from evidence, selecting out those data that confirm their initial beliefs.

Summary

Investigations of child welfare practice have not uncovered a constant set of principles that guide practitioners in making decisions. While worker decision-making behavior is constrained by resource deficits, by the fact that some decisions are made by others before a worker receives a case, and by practices within a given agency, failure to identify practice principles that govern the selection of options is distressing.

Decision making requires a framework for sorting data so that information that is relevant to a decision can be separated from that which is not pertinent. Information that is germane to any decision must be weighted in proportion to its significance for selecting an option. When the latter process yields equivocal results, professional judgment is applied to make a final decision.

Professional values and standards, the professional literature, statutory law, and agency policy should aid the decision-making process. Unfortunately, none of these sources has traditionally offered guidance that had direct applicability to practice. The breadth of the best interest of the child standard, the copious amounts of information that the professional literature directs workers to acquire, and the vagueness of statutory law may hinder, rather than facilitate, the decision maker's tasks. Until recently, agency policy that could be operationalized to assist the practitioner has been the exception. It is not surprising, therefore, that reliability in decision making is poor and that individual discretion and personal bias have been found to exert a strong influence on the decision-making behavior of child welfare staff.

Without guidance from professional standards, professional literature, statutory law, and agency policy, individual judgment will exert a strong influence at all stages of the decision-making process. But, in light of the evidence showing the degree to which individual bias influences the process of decision making, whether the judgmental strategies used can be viewed in the context of professional expertise is questionable.

Several judgmental tactics and their effects on decision-making behavior were reviewed. Information may be assigned to categories based on similarities between the object to be assigned and one's cognitive representations of members of different categories. This form of stereotyping, while functional for many day-to-day activities, causes problems for the professional when it is the only strategy used. Failure to consider the statistical probabilities that a client is a member of a given category—abusive or neglectful parent, for example—can lead to incorrect decisions which are based on superficial similarities between a client and the worker's cognitive representions of members of a class. If such an error is made, the likelihood of making further decisional errors increases. Once a person has been assigned to a category their future behavior is likely to be seen in light of categorical expectations.

Information that is available in memory affects judgments regarding the frequency and the probability of events as well as causal explanations of behavior. The likelihood that a worker's reservoir of information will be disproportionately negative is increased by the theories of human behavior that prevail in social work education and by practice experiences. There is an association between the vividness of information and the retrieval of data from memory. Thus, extremely negative cases of child abuse, about which workers are more likely to have information than cases where outcomes are positive, are apt to be more readily available for retrieval from memory, hence more likely to influence the decision-making process. Vividness of information also influences the weights that are assigned to data. More negative information is likely to be assigned greater weight than less negative information.

Theoretical assumptions regarding the causes of human behavior, which are influenced by professional as well as personal experiences, can exert an influence throughout the decision-making process. If theories are applied to situations without sufficient justification, if the decision maker believes that factual observations rather than biased theories such as those involved in stereotyping, are being used as guides, and if the existence of a theory precludes careful examination of data, additional sources of bias enter into the decision-making equation. The evidence showing that theoretical assumptions are often intractable in the face of contradictory evidence is reason for great concern.

Discussion

For the past two decades the child welfare system in the United States has been studied in depth, resulting in a barrage of criticism of all facets of the system.[44] Whether focusing on the individual and his or her decision-making or planning behavior or on the product of individual efforts with respect to outcomes for families and children or on the results of collective endeavors such as policies formulated, the picture that emerged was one of a system at odds with itself.

Efforts at reform ran in tandem with ongoing investigations and continued criticism of child welfare practices during the 1970s. It would not be an overstatement to say that significant changes are occurring at all levels of the child welfare system. For example, federal funding patterns, which in the past countered rather than reinforced the policy goals of supporting and maintaining family life, have been reformulated. The fiscal incentives associated with the Adoption Assistance and Child Welfare Act of 1980 are meant to ensure that the states will emphasize permanency for children with priority given to the maintenance of children in their own homes.[45] For those children who cannot remain with their families of origin, permanency through adoption is stressed. If the Congress allocates the funds necessary to reinforce policy objectives, state-level reform, which has already begun, can be expected to continue.

The changes that have taken place over the last decade go well beyond the passage of new policies to include the development and implementation of computerized information systems[46] as well as court or administrative review procedures to monitor the movement of children toward permanency goals.[47] Policies have also established requirements for substantive case planning for all children in care,[48] modification of termination statutes to ease the process of freeing children for adoption,[49] and reconceptualization of the roles of foster parents (with an emphasis on professionalizing their role),[50] biological parents and children (increasingly seen as partners in the planning process)[51] and workers (from that of treatment agent to that of decision-maker and case manager).[52]

These changes, taken together, create a framework for accountability that will severely curtail the autonomy of the practitioner. Of special concern are changes in the juvenile justice system and their implications for practice. While court decisions have been equivocal, the trend toward formalization of court procedures—the emerging due process orientation of the juvenile court—is clear. Following a brief review of this subject, the implications for practice are highlighted.

Formalizing Juvenile Court Procedures

Just as social work practice in child welfare has been subject to scrutiny and criticism, so have the practices of the juvenile court. Failure of the court to fulfill its rehabilitative mission has been the central criticism.[53] Changes that have occurred and those underway point to increasing the formality of juvenile court procedures and to strengthening the role of the court in monitoring the practices of child welfare agencies.

Evidence of this can be seen in the frequency with which children coming before the court are being granted due process rights such as the right to receive notice of a hearing, to cross-examine witnesses, and the right to counsel.[54] These changes have had their major impact on the jurisdictional phase of delinquency proceedings. With increasing frequency, they are also having an impact on neglect and dependency hearings. For example, a child's right to counsel has been recognized in some cases which seek to compel medical treatment or education, or to commit youngsters to mental hospitals.[55] Significant in this regard are "cases that have pitted children's rights against those of the child-caring agencies to make unilateral decisions for youngsters in their care. . . . These cases have challenged the doctrine of *in loco parentis* under which persons and institutions caring for children are said to occupy the legal position of the child's parent and, as such, to be immune from suit.[56] They have been successful in asserting a child's right to contest treatment, to receive treatment, and to be free of arbitrary punishment."[57]

The relationship between child welfare workers, foster parents, biological parents, and children is changing as the courts endeavor to ensure that the rights of all parties are respected in court hearings. The courts have shown a willingness to acknowledge that foster parents who have provided care for children over a period of years may have rights when custody decisions are made. Specifically, the concept of psychological parenthood[58] is gaining credence as courts show a willingness to grant standing to foster parents in custody hearings.

Likewise, the National Council of Juvenile and Family Court Judges is striving to ensure that practitioners actively involve a child's biological parents in the decision-making and planning process.[59] Judges are being admonished to query parents regarding their involvement in case planning, their understanding of the case plan, and their agreement with the goals and objectives that are established.[60]

"As juvenile court proceedings become more formal, uncorroborated admissions, hearsay testimony, and untested social investigations will no longer be acceptable as the basis for adjudication. Workers will be expected to present substantive, factual testimony in court. Therefore, guidelines for gathering and recording data during assessment, investigation, case planning, and service delivery will stress the acquisition of factual, rather than impressionistic, information and will emphasize recording in a descriptive, as opposed to an inferential manner. Workers will have to become familiar with legal rules regarding evidence in order to determine what to look for during investigations and what will be admissible in court."[61] If the American Bar Association's guidelines for presenting information to the court are adopted, the use of summary labels, without a descriptive account of the observed facts from which the labels were drawn, will not be permitted in court.

With regard to issues of evidence, it is noteworthy that in March 1982 the Supreme Court strengthened the evidentiary requirement for termination of parental rights cases from the less stringent "preponderance of the evidence" to a requirement for "clear and convincing evidence." The court "ruled that due process requires states to establish by clear and convincing evidence allegations supporting a petition to terminate parental rights."[62]

Earlier we said that all of the changes occurring in the child welfare system, which have been briefly outlined above, are creating a framework for accountability that will curtail the autonomy of the practitioner. The implications for decision making in practice are not difficult to discern. The decision maker whose case rests on personal values and idiosyncratic assumptions and whose conclusions are based on the use of intuitive decision-making strategies will be in great difficulty when called on to justify choices that are made. That practitioners need a structured framework for information gathering and decision making seems clear. The creation of a formal structure to monitor practice is not, however, the sole basis for this imperative. Professional ethics and social work's long-standing commitment to client self-determination demand a more rational, less subjective approach to selecting the options which have strong and enduring effects on the lives of the clients that are served.

Notes and References

1. Carol D. Austin, "Clinical Assessment in Context," *Social Work Research and Abstracts,* Vol. 17, No. 1 (Spring 1981), p. 8.

2. Ann W. Shyne and Anita G. Schroeder, National Study of Social *Services to Children and Their Families* (Washington, D.C.: United States Children's Bureau, DHEW Publication No. (OHDS) 78-30150, 1978), p. 78.

3. See, for example, Briar, op cit.; Shinn, op cit.; Jones et al., op cit.; Stein, *A Content Analysis,* op cit.; and Stein, Gambrill, and Wiltse, op cit.

4. Phillips et al., *Factors Associated with Placement* Decisions, op cit.

5. Alfred Kadushin, *Supervision in Social Work* (New York: Columbia University Press, 1976).

6. Phyllis Osborn, "Client Needs and the Manpower Shortage in Public Assistance and Child Welfare Services," *Education for Social Work, 1962 Proceedings* (New York: Council on Education for Social Work, 1962), pp. 106–115; Ernest N. Gullerud and Frank H. Itzin, "Continuing Education as an Effective Linkage Between Schools of Social Work and the Practice Community," *Journal of Education for Social Work,* Vol. 15, No. 3 (Fall 1979), p. 82; Theodore J. Stein, "Child Welfare: New Directions in the Field and Their Implications for Education," in *A Dialogue on the Challenge for Education and Training: Child Welfare Issues in the 80's,* ed. Ellen S. Saalberg (Ann Arbor, Michigan: National Child Welfare Training Center, 1982), pp. 57–76.

7. Richard Nisbett and Lee Ross, *Human Inference: Strategies and Shortcomings of Social Judgment* (Englewood Cliffs, New Jersey: Prentice-Hall, Inc., 1980), p. 7.

8. Daniel Kahneman and Amos Tversky, "On the Psychology of Prediction," *Psychological Review,* Vol. 80, No. 4 (1973), pp. 237–251; Amos Tversky and Daniel Kahneman, "Judgment Under Uncertainty: Heuristics and Biases," *Science,* Vol. 185 (September 1974), pp. 1124–1131.

9. Nisbett and Ross, op cit., p. 8.

10. Tversky and Kahneman, *Judgment Under Uncertainty,* op cit.; Daniel Kahneman and Amos Tversky, "Subjective Probability: A Judgment of Representativeness," *Cognitive Psychology,* No. 3 (1972), pp. 430–454; Amos Tversky and Daniel Kahneman, "Availability: A Heuristic for Judging Frequency and Probability," *Cognitive Psychology,* Vol. 5 (1973), pp. 207–232.

11. Nisbett, p. 7.

12. Tversky and Kahneman, op cit., pp. 1124–25; Amos Tversky and Daniel Kahneman, "Belief in the Law of Small Numbers," *Psychological Bulletin,* Vol. 76, No. 2 (1971), pp. 105–110.

13. The Advisory Committee on Child Development, *Toward a National Policy for Children and Families* (Washington, D.C.: National Academy of Sciences, 1976), p. 18.

14. Jeanne M. Giovannoni and Andrew Billingsley, "Family, One Parent," in *Encyclopedia of Social Work, Volume I,* eds. John B. Turner et al. (Washington, D.C.: National Association of Social Workers, 1977), p. 403.

15. Tversky and Kahneman, *Judgment Under Uncertainty,* op cit., p. 1125.

16. Brieland, *An Experimental Study,* op cit.

17. Tversky and Kahneman, op cit., p. 1126.

18. Theodore J. Stein, *Social Work Practice in Child Welfare* (Englewood Cliffs, New Jersey: Prentice-Hall, Inc., 1981), pp. 46–47.

19. Tversky and Kahneman, op cit., p. 1126.

20. Nisbett, op cit., p. 7.

21. Ibid.

22. Ibid.

23. Tversky and Kahneman, op cit., p. 1127.

24. Paul Slovic, Baruch Fischhoff, and Sarah Lichtenstein, "Risky Assumptions," *Psychology Today,* Vol. 14, No. 1 (June 1980), p. 45.

25. Tversky and Kahneman, op cit., p. 1128.

26. Leontine Young, *Wednesday's Children: A Study of Neglect and Abuse* (New York: McGraw Hill Book Company, 1964), p. 113; David Gil, *Violence Against Children: Physical Child Abuse in the United States* (Cambridge, Mass.: Harvard University Press, 1973), ch. 1.

27. Eileen D. Gambrill and Theodore J. Stein, *Supervision in Child Welfare: A Training Manual* (Berkeley, California: University of California Extension Press, 1978), p. 106.

28. Nisbett and Ross, op cit., p. 75.

29. Ibid., p. 57.

30. Cited in Mort LaBrecque, "On Making Sounder Judgments: Strategies and Snares," *Psychology Today,* Vol. 14, No. 1 (June 1980), p. 42.

31. Hogarth, *Judgment and Choice,* p. 4.

32. Nisbett, op cit., p. 172.

33. Ibid.

34. John I. Smith and E. Hocking, "Index of Concern: An Instrument for Use in Treatment of Cases of Physical Abuse of Children," *Child Abuse and Neglect: The International Journal,* Vol. 5, No. 3 (1981), p. 276. It seems reasonable to suggest that any single focus taken can create a bias that may negatively affect case outcomes. Thus, an overemphasis on strengths can result in missing important information regarding family weaknesses.

35. Cited in Mort, op cit., p. 39.

36. Nisbett, op cit., pp. 70,71.

37. Ibid., p. 244.

38. Ibid., p. 118.

39. Ibid., p. 169.

40. Ibid., p. 122.

41. Ibid., p. 123.

42. For a thorough discussion of this issue, see Walter Mischel, *Personality and Assessment* (New York: John Wiley and Sons, Inc., 1968).

43. See Nisbett, op cit., ch. 5.

44. Jane Knitzer, Mary Lee Allen, and Brenda McGowan, *Children Without Homes: An Examination of Public Responsibility to Children in Out-of-Home Care* (Washington, D.C.: The Children's Defense Fund, 1978).

45. *Adoption Assistance and Child Welfare Act,* op cit.

46. See *Children and Youth Centered Information System Data Advancement and Technical Assistance Newsletter,* published by CYSTEMS (Washington, D.C.: 1346 Connecticut Avenue Northwest).

47. The Adoption Assistance and Child Welfare Act of 1980 requires states to establish either a court or administrative review procedure. If states elect an administrative review procedure, the Act requires that it be "open to the participation of the parents of the child, conducted by a panel of persons at least one of whom is not responsible for the case management of, or the delivery of, services to either the child or the parents who are the subject of the review." See Adoption Assistance and Child Welfare Act, op cit., p. 11.

48. Ibid.

49. *Trends in Child Protection Laws—1977* (Denver, Colorado: Education Commission of the States, 1978), pp. 14–16.

50. *Standards for Foster Family Service Systems* (Washington, D.C.: American Public Welfare Association, March 1975), pp. 43–57.

51. Anthony Maluccio and Paula A. Sinanoglu, eds., *The Challenge of Partnership: Working with Parents of Children in Foster Care* (New York: Child Welfare League of America, 1981).

52. See June Axinn and Herman Levin, "Money, Politics and Education: The Case of Social Work," *History of Education Quarterly,* Vol. 18, No. 2 (Summer 1978), p. 144; Theodore J. Stein, "Macro and Micro Level Issues in Case Management," in *Case Management: State of the Art: Final Report* (Washington, D.C.: National Association of Social Workers, 1981), pp. 72–97.

53. Sanford N. Katz, "Introduction," in The Youngest Minority: Lawyers in Defense of Children, ed. Sanford N. Katz (Washington, D.C.: American Bar Association Press, 1974), pp. 17–19.

54. Roberta Gottesman, *The Child and the Law* (St. Paul, Minnesota: West Publishing Co., 1981), ch. 1.

55. Carol M. Rose, *Some Emerging Issues in Legal Liability of Children's Agencies* (New York: Child Welfare League of America, 1978).

56. Ibid., pp. 5–6, 8.

57. Ibid.

58. Ibid., p. 41; "Children's Rights Report," Vol. 1, No. 4 (New York: Juvenile Rights Project of the American Civil Liberties Union Foundation, December 1976–January 1977), pp. 4–5.

59. *Judicial Review of Children in Placement Deskbook* (Reno, Nevada: National Council of Juvenile and Family Court Judges, 1981).

60. Ibid., pp. 81–86. The deskbook also sets forth questions that judges should ask of foster parents and children as well as guidelines for review of the plan itself.

61. C. Bell and W. J. Mlyniec, "Preparing for a Neglect Proceeding: A Guide for the Social Worker," *Public Welfare,* Vol. 32, No. 4 (1974), pp. 26–37; Institute for Judicial Administration, American Bar Association, Juvenile Justice Standards Project, Standards Relating to Juvenile Records and Information Systems—Tentative Draft (Cambridge, Mass.: Ballinger Publishing Co., 1977), p. 71.

62. "Terminating the Parent-Child Relationship: Need for Clear and Convincing Evidence," *Children's Legal Rights Journal,* Vol. 3, No. 5 (March, April 1982), pp. 14–16.

4 A MODEL FOR DECISION MAKING

The model that we used to guide us in developing a framework for decision making is shown in figure 4-1.[1] The environmental context in which decisions are made consists of three domains: the social, professional, and program environments. The social environment includes a system of values which is articulated in social policy and statutory law. Values are given expression by legislators when they fund social programs through which child welfare services are provided. Professional values are inextricably linked with social values, if not wholly synonymous with them. Social science knowledge and the technology derived from that knowledge guide professional practice by providing a means for achieving program goals. While separable for purposes of discussion, the variables within the social, professional, and programmatic domains interact with each other.

The Social and Professional Environments

Major variables within the social and professional environments were reviewed in chapter 2, where professional values and standards, the professional literature, and statutory law were presented in the context of discussing sources of

35

Figure 4-1.   Decision Making Model*

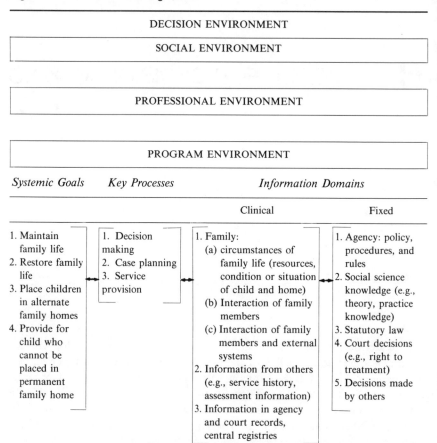

*This diagram represents a partial model. All of the variables external to the program environment are not shown. Political considerations that influence funding decisions are a notable omission.

guidance for decision making. (Agency policy, also covered in that discussion, is in the programmatic domain.) From that review, we concluded that these sources of guidance offer little in the way of assistance with direct application to decision making in practice situations.[2]

One of the first tasks that we confronted in developing guidelines for decision making was to operationalize, to the extent possible, the values expressed in the best interest of the child standard. Guidance for this task was found in the legal and social work literature in which the limits of the best interest test as a standard for decision making are set forth. In this literature, arguments are presented for an alternative standard for decision making and for delineating the statutory conditions that constitute abuse and neglect.[3]

The main criticisms of the best interest test include our inability to make long-range predictions, lack of social and professional consensus as to what is in any child's best interest, and the likelihood that use of this decision-making standard creates an artificial dichotomy between parents and children, thus detracting from the workers' main task which is to preserve the family unit. And, a child's caretaker has a right to know which of his or her behaviors are proscribed by law.[4] The ambiguity of abuse and neglect statutes permits discretionary decision making that encourages intervention under arbitrary conditions, hence failing to support this right.

An acceptable decision-making standard must lend itself to the development of operational criteria which can be applied reliably on a case-by-case basis to determine whether child care meets minimally acceptable standards and which lends itself to setting attainable goals. An acceptable standard for decision making should respect the ethnic and cultural diversity of any society by specifying minimum standards of child care below which most would agree that state intervention to protect a child is necessary, thus limiting individual discretion in decisions to intervene in family life. This is best accomplished if intervention decisions require evidence that a child has been harmed or is at risk of harm in the near future. This evidentiary requirement recognizes that efforts to make long-range predictions are not fruitful. Its use represents an effort to reduce the chances that intervention will occur for moral reasons alone.

If the decision maker focuses on minimum standards of parenting and is required to present evidence that children have been harmed or are at risk in the near future, we are more likely to serve the best interests of children where best interest is defined in relation to what is possible given the limits of knowledge at any time. A focus on minimum standards reinforces the value that most societies place on family privacy—on the right of parents to raise their children free from outside intervention—while simultaneously protecting a child's right to be safeguarded from undue harm as well as the right to be raised by the family of origin. The best interest standard leaves a wide margin for subjectivity and individual biases to influence decisions as to when intervention should occur, thereby undermining these values.

Moreover, parents are at risk of having their behavior evaluated against an ideal[5] that would not be found in the community-at-large. Even if ideals were attainable—if they could be translated into observable phenomena and if we had sufficient resources to attain them—intervention toward such ends would require a rethinking of our philosophy regarding the right of parents to raise their children free from outside interference.

A focus on minimum standards facilitates a description of the data base for decision making and the establishment of decision-making rules. For example, in many jurisdictions in the United States, statutory law permits intervention by child welfare agencies if parents are said to abuse controlled substances.[6] There is no requirement that evidence showing the effects on children be presented. Rather than being concerned solely with a parent's use of drugs or alcohol, we would require workers to answer the question How is the child being harmed by such behaviors or what harm might we expect to occur if substance abuse continues? Assessment would focus on the child's needs for supervision, medical care, education, shelter, and emotional support.

Consider the area of supervision. During assessment, workers' attention would focus on issues such as the child's self-help skills (e.g., her ability to dial an emergency telephone number, knowledge of how to cross the street, information that she has regarding who to turn to in the event of an emergency), the parent's knowledge of the child's ability to care for self and whether these are realistic in relation to the child's self-help skills, resources that are available to assist the youngster if the need for help should arise when the parent is not present (e.g., neighbors or relatives to whom the child can turn), and the availability and affordability of child-care resources such as day care. Information from any one of these areas would be viewed in relation to information from other areas and the decision made whether or not to intervene. (Additional examples of the application of an alternative standard are presented later in this chapter.)

The final argument in favor of revised standard for decision making is highlighted by recent evidence that suggests that in cases where failure to provide is the primary or sole allegation, poverty is a common factor.[7] Certainly, the development of an alternative standard of decision making and of new practice models cannot resolve intractable problems such as poverty. However, a decision-making standard focusing solely on specific harms to the child as the prerequisite for state intervention would reduce the chances of coercive intervention when poverty is the main source of a client's difficulties.

The Program Environment

The program environment is embedded in the social and professional environments. Program goals and the processes used to realize goals are derived from social values and social science knowledge. Practice knowledge should, in turn, feed into and expand the base of social science knowledge. The main elements of the program environment as they relate to decision making are described next.

Goals

The model shown in figure 4-1 is explicit in identifying the family unit, not the child in isolation, as the unit for service; hence this is the focal point around which all child welfare decisions must initially revolve. American law and social custom direct that biological parents have a right to the custody, care, and control of their children and all initial decision making must reinforce this right. When parental actions yield evidence that they cannot or will not continue to care for their children, attention must shift in the child's right to be raised in the continuous care of another set of adults. Thus, the model supports what has long been cited as goals of the child welfare system. In descending order, these are: maintaining family life through the provision of services to children in their own homes, restoring family life when children have been placed in out-of-home care, and the placement of children in permanent family homes through adoption or court appointment of a legal guardian when neither of the first two options is possible. Planned long-term foster care is an alternative, although a less desirable one given the absence of legal safeguards for such arrangements.

These goals provide a reference point against which the decision maker must evaluate or balance all choices. Stated otherwise, each time a decision is made the decision maker must ask the question To what extent will this particular alternative further attainment of a systemic goal? For example, when a child enters out-of-home care (assuming that the youngster does not have special needs that require placement in a residential treatment facility) the decision where to place, when made in the context of the goal of restoring family life, may force a different set of choices than when the goal centers primarily on the child's well-being. The former goal narrows the range of alternatives by focusing the decision maker's attention on selecting a placement that is geographically proximate to the child's biological parents since we know that parental visiting is a key variable in restoration.[8] Since a majority of parents served by child welfare agencies are poor and presumably unable to afford costly transportation and assuming that there is an inverse relationship between the probability of frequent visits and the distances to be traveled to a visiting site, it is possible to rank order placement alternatives based on their geographic proximity to the home of biological parents.

Selecting an initial placement, where the concern is solely with the child's needs, may result in choices that militate against family reunification. This may be justified if there is persuasive evidence that the child has special needs which cannot be met in the community where the parent resides. In considering whether the child's needs demand a special placement, the hypothetical costs in terms of long-range goals must be taken into consideration. Decisions based primarily on the child's well-being may be correct once evidence shows that reunification is not possible, in which case the decision maker directs her attention to finding an alternative permanent home for the child.

Key Processes

Our position is that managing information in order to reach decisions that will result in permanency in a child's living arrangements, and formulating these decisions into case plans, the objectives of which are realized through the provision of services, are, in that order, the key processes through which systemic goals are attained. The suggestion that decision making to achieve permanency is the key process differs markedly from the position that treatment and nurturance of children are the main objectives of child welfare.[9] Treatment to remediate the conditions that led to a family's involvement with a child caring agency is clearly necessary; however, in this model treatment is in the service of decision making, not an end in itself. Thus, given a goal of family reunification and recognizing the relationship between the probabilities of attaining this outcome and the length of time a child is in care,[10] the range of problems that concern a child welfare worker and the level of family change which must occur to restore a child, will be set in relation to the primary objective of family reunification. This places a ceiling on the change demands that child welfare workers can make of parents, supporting a focus on minimal standards of parenting.

This position should not be construed as suggesting that families be left with unresolved difficulties. It does, however, suggest that public child welfare agencies are only one part of a community's system for serving families, and that distinctions must be made between the objectives of public child caring agencies and other community systems, family service agencies, and community mental health, for example. If such distinctions are not made, the current practice of using public child caring agencies as a dumping ground for cases that other community agencies do not want to serve is reinforced. The irony of this should be readily apparent. Child welfare staff, given their reliance on community agencies to assist in resolving family difficulties, are put in the position of having to refer families to the very community agencies that rejected them and referred them to child welfare in the first place.

The focus on limiting the range of problems that are the proper concern of child welfare agencies and on setting limits to the changes we demand of families, places boundaries on which aspects of a client's life-space are the proper subject for inquiry which a treatment model leaves open-ended. Setting boundaries is critical if criteria to guide practitioners in their data-collection and decision-making activities are to be specified, such guidance following from knowledge of how information will be used. Additionally, a respect for family privacy demands that workers justify their information-gathering activities. Again, such justification comes from knowledge of how information will be used. Also, time constraints, imposed by caseload size and administrative paper work demand that limits be set. Finally, approximately 75 percent of the children in the care of public welfare agencies are being served by persons with no academic training in social work. Sixteen percent of the 25 percent with social work degrees hold bachelor's degrees, only 9 percent graduate degrees.[11] Thus, even if a treatment model was appropriate in the past, the realities of current practice indicate that this is no longer the case.

Information

The model identifies two information domains. The first is labeled clinical, the second, fixed. Information in the clinical domain requires worker judgment in deciding which items of information, out of a defined range, are relevant to any case, how best to gather relevant information, and how it is to be interpreted. Fixed information remains relatively constant over the life of any case although it may change over time. Agency policy and court decisions such as those dealing with a client's right to treatment, are examples.

Fixed information in the programmatic domain, such as agency policy, statutory law, and court decisions, will reflect regional differences. In the United States, for instance, federal policy establishes certain requirements which each state must meet to receive federal funds. But, the states have latitude in interpreting federal policy to the varying conditions found in the states. Likewise, statutory law and court decisions may vary across states. This highlights the fact that certain elements of any framework for decision making are subject to modification to take account of regional differences.

The central point that we are making in identifying two information domains is that decision making in child welfare is rarely, if ever, a wholly clinical phenomenon in the sense that decisions made by private practitioners may be. From the worker's standpoint, there is continual interaction between these two domains wherein fixed information sets limits to the options the worker may select. Some states, for example, preclude intervention for emotional abuse. If parents refuse assistance, a worker may have to withdraw from a case even if he has evidence that the child has emotional problems.

Dichotomizing information into clinical and fixed domains and identifying the variables in each domain facilitates the development of decision criteria. For example, if the decisions that workers make are isolated and each decision viewed in relation to clinical and fixed information domains, the general data base for the decision can be identified. The data base for some decisions, eligibility for services, for instance, may be derived solely from agency policy. For other decisions, clinical and fixed domains must be viewed in tandem. In the remainder of this chapter, examples of the decision-making procedures that we developed and tested in the Illinois/West Virginia Project are presented.

Decision-making Procedures—Some Examples

For purposes of our project, intake was defined as a process that begins with an initial request for services or a report of abuse or neglect and continues through development of a service plan. We identified nine clinical decisions that could be made for each case.[12] These are: (1) Is an emergency response necessary?[13] (2) Is the child in immediate danger? (3) Can the child be safeguarded at home or is protective custody necessary? (4) Is there credible evidence of abuse or neglect? (5) Is assistance required with the investigation or assessment process? (6) Is it necessary to petition the court? (7) Will the child be left at home or placed in foster care? (8) What are the specific problems for which services are necessary? and (9) What is the most appropriate case plan?

Some of the decisions identified may not reflect options available to workers in some jurisdictions. Policy or law may require staff to petition the court anytime there is evidence of maltreatment or anytime a child is removed from the care of his or her parents.

For each decision, flow charts showing the process that workers follow to make the decision of concern were developed. Questions that arise in the process of making each decision are bordered by diamonds. Directives for staff action are bordered by rectangles. Figure 4-2 can be used to illustrate how to read a flow chart.

When cases first come to reception, workers must determine the client's status in the agency. Whether the case is active is one of the first questions that an intake worker must address. If it is, a referral is made to the supervisor or worker handling the case. A negative answer to this question gives rise to a series of questions as shown. The process followed by the intake worker will differ as a function of whether each of the remaining questions is answered

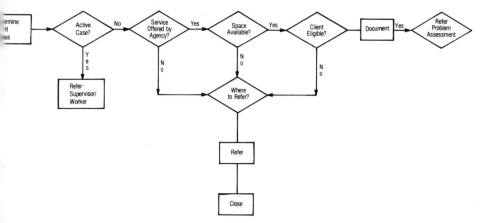

URE 4-2. Sample Flow Chart

affirmatively or negatively. Regardless of the answer, all courses of action shown in the flow chart culminate in a directive. Some directives result in closing cases to the agency, others draw attention to the next stage of the intake process. For example, when the question "Is the client eligible?" is answered in the affirmative, workers are directed to document certain items of information and to refer the case for problem assessment. A negative answer to the question requires workers to decide where to refer the case subsequent to which it is closed to the agency.

The materials presented in the following pages were used to train child welfare staff for the field test of the Illinois/West Virginia Project. These materials, formatted in a training manual, were used by staff to guide them in making decisions during the field test. The portion of the training manual that follows is abstracted in its entirety to give the reader an understanding of the guidelines that were available to staff during the field test. Guidelines for making four decisions are presented. These are: Is an immediate home visit necessary? Is assistance needed with the investigation? Is the child in immediate danger and, if so, can the child be safeguarded at home or is protective custody necessary? and Is there credible evidence of abuse or neglect?

Reception[14]

The first decision at protective service reception is whether an immediate home visit is necessary.[15] Most states allow 24 to 48 hours following receipt of a report for the investigation to begin. But there are situations in which the information provided by the reporter suggests that a child is in imminent danger warranting an immediate response, say within an hour or two of the time a report is received.

Figure 4-3 shows the process that a protective service reception worker follows from the time that a report is received through the decision whether the situation warrants an emergency response.

The reception worker's first task is to document the information provided by the reporter. This information is the basic data for determining whether an immediate home visit is necessary. Four categories of information are elicited from reporters. The data elements shown in each category are a sample of items recorded.

The subject family is identified by name, address, and telephone number; the age of the child who is the subject of the report is recorded as is the parent's primary language. The reception worker asks for the name of the child's school, the child's teacher, the name and address of the family doctor or local clinic, and whether the reporter can identify others who may have information that is pertinent to the report.

The reason for the report, the child's whereabouts at the time of the report, when the incident being reported came to the caller's attention, and how often the events being reported were observed are recorded next. It is important to learn whether the reporter has (a) first-hand knowledge of the events being described. For example, did the reporter observe a child being beaten, hear a

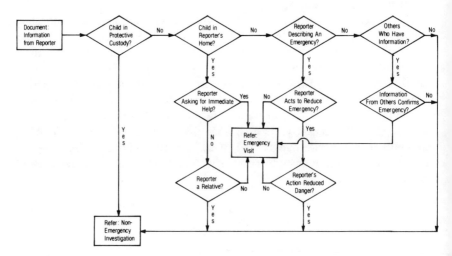

FIGURE 4-3.   Is an Immediate Home Visit Necessary?

child crying for a prolonged period of time, or did the child tell the reporter that she is afraid to return home? (b) Second-hand knowledge where the caller is describing events reported to him or her by another person (e.g., a neighbor) of which he or she has no firsthand knowledge; or (c) is reporting impressions as might be the case when the caller states "I think that something is wrong because I have not seen the child for several days."

The reception worker formulates questions to ascertain the source of the caller's information, such as Please tell me what you saw or heard? or How did you acquire the information that you are reporting? Data is recorded using direct quotes when possible.

The reporter is described next, including organizational affiliation if the person is a professional. Since the laws of many states allow reporters to remain anonymous, the reception worker may not be able to elicit information in this category. However, the reporter may be the only person with first hand knowledge of maltreatment and the evidence that he or she can offer may be crucial to sustaining allegations of abuse or neglect. Thus, the caller is told that his or her willingness to be identified and interviewed by the investigatory worker is important. But, the caller's wish to remain anonymous must be respected.

Whether the reporter told the parents that a report was being made and, if so, how the parents responded are the final items of information elicited.

Using Information for Decision Making

The information provided by the reporter must be reviewed and a decision made whether to respond immediately. The order in which information is elicited from reporters is important. Starting with identification of the subject family allows a protective service response should the caller have a change of heart and hang up the telephone before all of the requisite information is obtained.

The child's whereabouts at the time of the report can determine whether immediate action is warranted. Children in protective custody are safe, precluding the need for immediate action. If the child is in the reporter's home and the reporter is asking that a representative of the agency pick up the youngster or states that child is ill or injured the worker knows that the case must be referred for an immediate home visit.

Whether the reporter is related to the child can have implications for deciding how quickly to respond. In some jurisdictions, if the reporter is a relative and is not asking for immediate help, state law permits the relative to retain custody of the child overnight. Immediate action is not required. In some states the child cannot remain in the reporter's home overnight unless the person is a relative or licensed foster parent. Thus, familiarity with the laws of the state in which one is practicing is necessary to determine action under these conditions.

If the reporter is describing an emergency situation, for example, the caller states that she observed a child being beaten or heard a child's life being threatened, emergency action is warranted unless the reporter acts to reduce the emergency. For example, a reporter may call a child indoors who is playing in a dangerous area or tell the child who cannot gain access to his own home to come into the reporter's home. Or, the caller may be willing to tell the child's parents what she observed. When the reporter describes an emergency situation, the receptionist asks the caller if she is willing to take action to reduce the danger reported if the action would not require the reporter to intervene between parent and child. Reporters should not be encouraged to act if they are hesitant to do so. When the caller agrees to act, the reception worker states that he will call back in 15 to 20 minutes to learn what happened. If danger has been reduced, a nonemergency response should suffice. Otherwise, a referral for immediate help is made.

There are situations where the contents of the report suggest the need for immediate action but do not clearly indicate that this is necessary. The contents of the report may be impressionistic. The caller might say that he thinks that something is wrong because he has not seen the child for several day or report that the child appears to be ill or injured but be unable to describe the child's condition. Hence, the reception worker may not be able to draw conclusions about the likelihood of danger.

Should this occur, an effort is made to contact others who may have information with utility for decision making. If the family's physician or local clinic can be contacted and if the child received medical attention, an immediate response may be avoided. Here, we assume that if the child were in danger the medical person would have made the report and would not have released the youngster to his parents. Or, if school is in session, the youngster's teacher may be contacted to learn if the child attended class that day. If so, it is likely that injuries serious enough to require immediate attention would have been observed and reported.

If the reporter is describing events that took place several hours before the call was made, the question Why have you waited until now to make this report? is asked. The answer to this question may determine the immediacy of response when the contents of the report are suggestive but not conclusive. If the caller's explanation for the delay seems reasonable, e.g., he says that he did not know what to do and just found out where to make the report or he states that he was not able to leave his home to go to a phone booth because he was caring for his own children, the suggestion that immediate action is necessary is plausible.

But, reporters may contradict themselves. A caller may describe a situation that appears to be an emergency and, at the same time, explain a delay by reporting that the situation did not seem urgent. Here too, the suggestion that workers contact others who may have relevant information is pertinent.

When information from a reporter is inconclusive and significant others cannot be contacted for additional data, workers must exercise professional judgment to determine whether an immediate response is needed. Since children may be at risk without medical attention it may be best to err on the side of caution by initiating an immediate visit anytime a lay reporter describes a child who seems to be injured or ill or who is in a situation that suggests possible danger.

Criteria for an Immediate Home Visit

(1) A reporter defines the situation as an emergency and there is no contradictory information from other sources.

(2) A reporter provides information leading the reception worker to hypothesize that an emergency situation exists. For example, the reporter states that she observed a child being beaten; a child attempting to gain access to her own home; a child whose dress is inappropriate for the weather so as to suggest that the youngster may become ill. Or, the reporter heard a child yelling or screaming for a prolonged period of time or overheard a child being threatened by a caretaker or other person and a parent is not present to whom the child can turn for help.

(3) A reporter states that a child has fled from his home and is afraid to return home *or* a child makes a report and states that he is afraid to return home.

(4) If the situation reported suggests danger (for example, because a child is playing in a heavily trafficked area where danger could be reduced if the child were called indoors) and the reporter has not indicated an unwillingness to speak with the parent or an inability to locate the parent, ask the reporter if she is willing to inform the parent of the child's situation. If yes, ask that she do so.

Ask the reporter if they would be willing to call the child indoors if a parent cannot be located. Tell the reporter that you will call back in 15 to 20 minutes to learn what happened. If the child is indoors, refer for a nonemergency investigation.

If the caller does not have a home phone, *or* if they cannot locate a parent or are not willing to try, *and* a young child can be heard crying or is observed to be in a dangerous situation *and* if the caller told the child to come indoors or to play elsewhere and the child will not listen *or* the caller refuses to take action, the case should be referred for an immediate home visit.

In Addition to the Above, Immediate Action May Be Avoided If:

(1) A physician or qualified medical person can be reached by telephone; the child has received medical attention and medical opinion is that an emergency response is not necessary.

(2) A youngster is of school age and the school can be contacted to learn if the child attended classes that day. If so, it is reasonable to assume that serious injuries would have come to the attention of a school authority. Even if they did not, the fact that the youngster went to school hints at the possibility that injuries are not so severe as to warrant immediate action.

(3) A person with firsthand information can be contacted (when the initial report was based on secondhand information) and the information provided indicates that an immediate visit is not necessary.

Bear in mind that an investigation occurs within 24 to 48 hours in nonemergency situations, and that older children are able to take certain actions on their own behalf.

Is Assistance Needed With the Investigation?   Many of the clients served by child welfare agencies have problems where assessment is beyond the skills of one person. The expertise of medical personnel, attorneys, psychologists, and psychiatrists, in addition to those of the child welfare worker, may be needed to determine whether a child is in immediate danger, the exact nature of client problems, and to select appropriate interventions. This decision may be made at protective services reception or by the worker who will initiate the investigation. For example, if a reporter states that a child has been injured, a worker may ask that a public health nurse accompany her on the home visit to examine the child and to determine whether medical attention is necessary. A relatively inexperienced worker may request assistance with basic investigatory procedures with which she is unfamiliar. The decision to request assistance may be made at a later time. Based on observations made during a first home visit, a worker may ask for diagnostic assistance from a psychologist or determine that it is necessary to take the child for a physical examination.

This decision may be reconsidered at later stages of a case based on the worker's observations and information provided during a home visit. Supervisory approval should be obtained prior to involving others in the assessment process.

The Investigation

When the investigation begins the worker's foremost concern is with the safety of each child in the home. If there is evidence of danger, whether children can be safeguarded at home or must be taken into protective custody has to be determined. The issues that concern protective service staff in reaching these decisions are shown in figure 4-4.

The worker responsible for the investigation receives the information that was recorded by the reception worker including a recommendation whether an immediate home visit is necessary. If immediate action is called for and assistance with the investigation is needed, a request for aid must be put forth.

Information from a variety of sources can contribute to the decisions made during the investigation. Some information can be gathered before the first home visit if immediate action is not required; other information cannot be obtained until the worker meets with the family. In the former category is data logged in the state's central registry such as prior reports on the family, data found in agency files, and information from collateral resources whose names were given to the reception worker or whose names appear in case records.

All of the services that a family has used or is currently using may not be identified in records. Since information from service providers can contribute to decision making, workers will question family members to learn about resources used.

The following illustrates how information that is retrieved from records or gained from collaterals can influence decisions. From information gathered during the investigation it is not always possible to determine conclusively whether a child has been harmed or is in danger. For example, a worker responding to a report that a young child is not being supervised may find a parent at home when she arrives. The child may be unharmed and the parent may deny having left the youngster alone. If the substance of the report cannot be confirmed, there may be no choice but to close the case. But if there are prior confirmed reports, similar in nature to the report under investigation, these can strengthen a weak case since they suggest a pattern of supervisorial neglect. It is important to know whether your state expunges unconfirmed reports. If not, information logged in the central registry may have little utility for decision making. Prior reports may reflect attempts to harass a family who does not conform to community standards but whose behavior is not harmful to children.

Collateral resources may have knowledge of a family that is useful for decision making. A mental health counselor may have diagnostic information showing that a child is suffering from emotional problems. The counselor's records may indicate that the child's parents have not followed through with

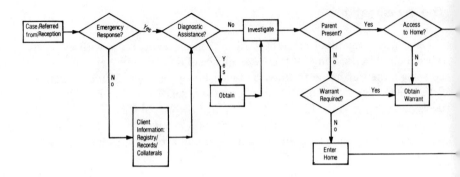

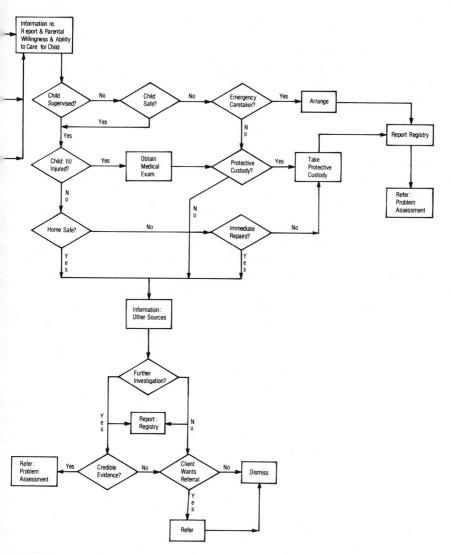

FIGURE 4-4.   Is Child in Immediate Danger? Can Child be Safeguarded at Home or Is Protective Custody Necessary?

a recommended plan for treatment. This information could be used to support a claim that the youngster is being emotionally neglected or abused.

Note that in both examples the suggestion that a child has been mistreated takes into account parental actions as well as the child's situation or condition. If the parent of an unsupervised child arranged for child care or accepted a worker's help in making arrangements and the parent whose child has emotional problems followed a recommended treatment plan, there would not be a basis for alleging neglect or abuse.

A worker begins the investigation by describing the nature of the report to the family (while maintaining the confidentiality of the reporting source) and the state law that requires the investigation. If entry to the home is denied, action must be taken that will result in observing and speaking to the parents and children since the question Are the children safe? must be answered. The action taken depends on state law. Some jurisdictions require that a warrant be obtained to gain entry to the home. In others, police and/or social service personnel are empowered to enter the home without a warrant when they are responding to a report of maltreatment.

The conditions under which the investigation takes place are strained. Parents may be nervous or frightened when apprised of the report whether or not they have mistreated their child. If a child has been abused or neglected, fear of discovery may condition parental behavior during this process. One must remain cognizant of the fact that some of the behaviors proscribed by abuse and neglect statues may be considered appropriate methods of child-rearing from the parents' viewpoint.

For example, spanking a child using a belt or other object may be a long-standing practice in some families. Laws proscribing such behavior have been enacted only recently.[16] Their passage cannot be expected to quickly modify well-established behavior patterns. Educating parents about child abuse laws, helping them to see how their behaviors deviate from the law, informing them of the legal consequences of continuing to engage in proscribed behaviors, and linking parents with service providers, who can help them learn new methods of child-rearing are major services provided by protective service personnel.

Decisions regarding danger to children and questions of whether those who are in danger can be protected at home must be made quickly, under what can be viewed as crisis circumstances. Parental cooperation may be minimal, the child's response fearful, and the worker an uninvited guest. The situation may constitute an actual crisis. Therefore, workers must make a series of rapid observations. Information must be elicited from family members, evaluated and used for on-the-spot decision making without benefit of supervisory consultation. Staff cannot expect to gather detailed data nor to undertake a rigorous evaluation of data. At best, one acquires a general level of information, such as whether a child appears to be harmed, rather than detailed information descriptive of the exact type of harm. Information detail is gathered at a later time. For these reasons, the guidelines for deciding whether a child is in immediate danger and, if so, whether protective custody is necessary must be commanded to memory if they are to be useful during the investigation.

Guidelines for Determining Whether a Child Is in Immediate Danger and, if so, Whether Protective Custody is Necessary

The following guide to decision making primarily is directive. Each of three parts contains instructions to guide action if a child is: (1) found unsupervised (Part I); (2) injured or ill (Part II); or (3) living in a home that is physically unsafe (Part III). All three sections are not necessarily relevant to every investigation. The contents of the report should suggest which section or sections are pertinent. If a reporter states that a child was beaten, attention is directed to Part II which deals with the child's physical condition. Questions regarding supervision and conditions of the home are not of immediate concern.

I. Supervision

1. *Is There an Adult in the Home?*
   (a) *If no*, go to question 2.
   (b) *If yes*, determine the caretaker's relationship to the child. If the caretaker is not the child's parent ask whether they are in the home by arrangement with the parent, whether they are willing to provide care until the parent returns home, and when the parent is expected home. Ask where the parent is and obtain a telephone number where she or he can be reached, if possible.
   (c) Does the caretaker seem able to care for the child? (Is her speech coherent? Is the caretaker able to discuss the child's supervision or does her train-of-thought wander, evidenced by incomplete sentences and difficulties in understanding what you are saying, assuming that difficulties are not a function of language differences?)
   (d) If the caretaker is the child's parent and seems unable to care for the child but will accept help, ask if there is a neighbor or relative you might call to provide assistance. If so, arrange for help. If not, send an emergency caretaker into the home. If the caretaker is not a child's parent, is not able to care

for the youngster or is unwilling to do so, try to locate a parent by telephone or by going to nearby homes. If a parent is located, ask that she return home immediately. Unless the parent returns while you are there, send an emergency caretaker into the home. If the caretaker is not able to provide care, if the caretaker will not accept help, or if emergency caretaker services are not available, take the child into protective custody.

(e) If the caretaker is not a parent but is able and willing to care for the child and is willing to do so and is in the home by arrangement with the parent, there is no reason to assume danger. The parent should be informed of the report. Further action is not warranted unless there are prior reports regarding supervision.

(f) If the parent or caretaker prevents you from seeing the child explain that, by law, you will have to request police assistance to determine whether the child is all right. If the parent or caretaker still refuses to let you see the youngster, enlist the aid of a police officer. Further action will be contingent upon what you observe in relation to the child's condition and conditions of the home (see Parts II and III).[17]

(g) If the caretaker or parent is verbally nonresponsive and/or physically unable to move, call for emergency medical assistance. Take the child into protective custody.

(h) If the parent or caretaker is bedridden but is able to discuss the child's supervision and condition, ask how the youngster is being supervised, fed, sent to school, and so forth. Inquire into the nature of the caretaker's illness and whether they have received medical attention.

(1) If the caretaker or parent seems able to provide supervision, for example, she or he can observe the child at play, is able to get out of bed should the child need help, is able to feed the child or the child is able to feed himself, and there is food in the house (or if you can obtain food) further action at this time is not warranted. A return visit within 48 hours to see how the family is managing is called for.

(2) Absent these conditions, have arrangements been made for a neighbor or relative to provide aid? If so, ask for permission to speak with the person to confirm her willingness to help. If the parent or caretaker will not cooperate, tell her that you will have to take the child into protective custody. If you can confirm the availability of help, further action is not warranted.

(3) If help has not been arranged, is there a relative or neighbor who can come to the home to provide assistance or to whose home the child can be brought? If so, and the parent or caretaker is agreeable to your making arrangements for help, do so.

(4) If a caretaker is not available, or help is not accepted, the child should be taken into protective custody.

(5) If the parent or caretaker has not received medical attention, ask if she would like you to arrange for it.

2. Did you find an infant alone?

(a) If no, go to question 3.

(b) If yes, try to locate a parent by asking a neighbor. If a parent is located or can be contacted by telephone, arrange for immediate supervision.

(c) If a parent cannot be found, ask the neighbor if she would be willing to supervise the infant until the parent returns home. Unless the neighbor is a relative or licensed foster parent, emergency supervision should not last overnight unless the person is willing to stay with the child in the child's home. If you arrange for supervision, give the neighbor/relative a telephone number where you or an agent of the agency can be reached.

(d) If immediate supervision cannot be arranged, send an emergency caretaker into the home. Otherwise, take the infant into protective custody.

3. Was a preschool child found alone?

(a) If no, go to question 4.

(b) If yes, ask the child if she knows how to locate her parent(s) or if she was given instructions about what to do if help is needed.

(c) If the child has instructions, for example, to contact a nearby relative or neighbor, you should telephone that person or go to that home to learn about the child care arrangements made.

(d) If an adult is located, arrange for immediate supervision. Otherwise, send an emergency caretaker into the home or, if none is available, take the child into protective custody.

4. Was a school-age child found alone?

(a) If no, go to question 5.

(b) If yes, follow the instructions under question 3, b and c.

(c) If an adult cannot be located, but the child is inside the home or has access to the home, ask the child if he knows when the parent is expected home and if he minds being alone until the parent returns.

(d) If the child has access to the indoors, knows when a parent will return, and does not express fear at being alone, ask the child what she would do if a fire started, if she felt ill, or became fearful. If the child has the telephone number of a family physician or nearby clinic, an emergency number such as 911, or was told to dial the operator to ask for help, an hypothesis of immediate danger is not warranted.

Give the youngster a telephone number where you or other agency representatives can be reached. Tell the child to telephone you if her parent does not return. Leave a note for the parent describing why you were at the home and instructing the parent to telephone you as soon as she returns. Indicate your intention to return to the home if a call is not received. Emergency action can be deferred.

(e) If the youngster is afraid to be alone or if there is no phone in the home or nearby neighbor to whom the child can turn for help, send an emergency caretaker into the home. Otherwise, take the child into protective custody.

(f) If the parent does not telephone you as instructed, a return home visit is called for. If the child is still alone, send an emergency caretaker into the home. Otherwise, take the child into protective custody.

5. Was a young child left in the care of an older sibling?
(a) If no, go to Part II: Child's Condition.
(b) If yes, follow through with the instructions for locating a parent under question 3, b and c. If a parent cannot be located, but the child knows when her parent will return, a dangerous situation should not be assumed.
(c) The older child's self-help skills should be assessed in the manner suggested under item d, question 4. The instructions under e and f, question 4 should be followed.

II. Child's Condition

1. Did you observe burns, lacerations, bruises, welts, or other signs of injury on the child's body?

2. Does a child appear to be ill, e.g., is he in bed? Is he feverish?

3. Did a child tell you that she or he is in pain?
Negative answers to these questions should direct your attention to the child's overt behavior for a clue as to whether there may be internal injuries. Internal injuries should affect the child's ability to talk, to play, or to move about when asked to.
(a) If no to the above questions, go to Part III. Conditions of the Home.
(b) If yes to any of these questions, is there evidence that the child has received medical attention? Evidence could take the form of a statement from a parent that a child was seen by a physician or public health nurse, bandages applied to a wound, a prescription with the child's name bearing a date that corresponds to the investigation/report, and/or written instructions from a medical person as to how the parent is to minister to the child.
(c) If the parent says that the child has received medical attention, obtain

the name, address, and telephone number of the medical person or clinic where the child was seen. Ask the parent's permission to contact the person or facility for information on the child's illness or injury.

(d) If the parent will not provide this information or refuses permission for you to contact the medical person, they should be told that, under law, you will have to arrange for an immediate medical examination.

If you have the name of a medical person, contact should be made as soon as possible. Further protective service action will be contingent upon the information you receive. If information from a medical person confirms the parent's report and there is no suggestion that the injury was deliberately inflicted, further action is not warranted.

If the medical report is discrepant with that of the parent, ask what the physician or nurse thinks needs to be done. We must assume that if the injury or illness were life-threatening or if there were evidence of deliberate intent to harm, that the child would not have been released to the parent. Therefore, an hypothesis of immediate danger is not warranted.

(e) If there is no evidence that the child has received medical attention, is there evidence that the parent has ministered to the child? For example, has salve been applied to a burn? Is there a bandage on a wound? Does the parent state that he is giving a child aspirin to bring down a fever?

(f) If the parent is attending to the child's illness and the child does not appear to be seriously ill (for instance, the child is able to speak to you in a manner that is coherent for his or her age, or is sitting up in bed playing with toys or watching television) emergency action is not called for. However, if the parent does not have a family doctor or access to medical facilities (and a Medicaid card if appropriate) the name, address, and telephone number of the nearest clinic, hospital, or public health facility should be provided. If the parent wishes, arrangements should be made for a public health nurse to visit the home or for transportation to take the child to a medical facility for an examination.

(g) If the child has not received medical attention and/or the parent has not made an effort to minister to the child, and, in your best judgment, the injury or illness seems serious, arrange for immediate medical attention.

4. If the child has been injured, regardless of severity, immediate medical attention is called for if:

(a) The parent will not explain how an injury was sustained.

(b) The parent's and child's explanations differ.

(c) The parent's explanation is not congruent with your observations, for example, lacerations on a child's back are explained as an accidental injury.

(d) The child is so withdrawn such that she or he will not respond to your questions and will not approach you or her/his parent.

(1) The parent should be asked to take the child to the nearest clinic or emergency room immediately. A representative of the agency should accompany the parent. If a parent will not take a child for an examination, the child should be taken into protective custody and examined by a medical person. Further action would be contingent upon the outcome of the medical examination.

5. The child should be taken into protective custody following a medical examination, if:

(a) There is evidence that physical abuse or nutritional neglect is so severe as to be life-threatening. Even if an injury is not severe;

(b) If there was an intent to kill the child, evidence by poisoning or assault with a deadly weapon, or if a child was repeatedly beaten with an object, or;

(c) There is evidence of abuse or neglect which, if not attended to, can be hypothesized to threaten the child's life, and the parent refuses help.

(d) When there is medical evidence of repeated abuse. For example, x rays show prior injuries that were not medically treated and which a medical person suggests could not have been sustained by accident.

(e) Any recurrence of severe abuse or neglect after services were offered.

(f) When there is psychiatric or psychological evidence of extreme behavioral disturbance or withdrawl by the child and the parent rejects the child.

(g) Evidence suggest that parent is not competent. For instance, a medical person states that the parent does not understand instructions for ministering to the child, and assuming that nonunderstanding is not a function of language differences and there are no resources such as family, friends, or emergency caretaker/homemaker services to help in the home while assessment is undertaken.

(h) If a child has been raped by a related adult or nonrelated adult known to the parent and the parent did not attempt to protect the child.

III. Conditions of the Home

1. The following list describes conditions of the family home that require action by protective services.

(a) The outside temperature is below 50° F. and there is no heat in the home.

(b) There are broken windows with jagged edges of glass.

(c) There is exposed electrical wiring.

(d) Bathroom facilities are not in working order.

(e) There are rotten floorboards in the home.

(f) There are holes in the roof through which rain or snow can enter the home.

(g) There is garbage/feces in the home which, in your opinion, pose a health hazard.

(h) There are rats in the home.

Any of these conditions may pose a threat to the entire family. Neglect should not be assumed unless the parent owns the home and refuses to make repairs they can afford or unless the parent refuses assistance from the agency. Efforts should be made to have repairs undertaken or to relocate the entire family. The child should be removed if parents will not cooperate.

If repairs can be made immediately or prior to the point at which they are likely to cause danger (for example, a broken furnace can be repaired before winter), arrangements for the repairs should be made. Follow up to ensure that necessary repairs were made.

If conditions cannot be improved in time to avert danger, the parent should be asked if there is a neighbor or relative with whom the family can stay until repairs are made or new housing found. If there are no safe alternatives for the entire family, the child should be placed in an emergency shelter until alternative living arrangements can be made for the entire family.

Worker observations in the three areas reviewed above are summarized on a checklist (figure 4-5) immediately after the home visit, before specific facts are forgotten or modified by memory. If protective custody was taken, the reasons are also indicated on the checklist. The ways in which workers determine what further action, if any, is necessary, are reviewed later in this section.

Determining Whether There Is Credible Evidence of Abuse or Neglect

Possible outcomes of the first home visit are to close the case when there is no basis for continuing the investigation, referring clients for assistance when requested; open the case if there is credible evidence of abuse or neglect; or continue the case for further investigation. In this section, we will review the process workers follow to determine which course of action to take. We will look at sources of information that contribute to decision making; the different types of evidence workers gather; and how information is used to determine whether there is evidence of maltreatment.

To begin, we want to stress the importance of workers familiarizing them-

FIGURE 4-5. Checklist: Observations from First Home Visit

INSTRUCTIONS: Record your observations on the following checklist by checking yes or no to each item. If a child was taken into protective custody, indicate why in Part IV. Use the narrative section at the end to summarize your observations, to clarify your actions, and to recommend further steps (e.g., arrange for psychological testing, request information from collaterals). If your observations suggest that the investigation should be closed, place a check mark in the box to the left. Explain your reasoning in the narrative.

☐

I. SUPERVISION

	YES	NO
1. Supervision was an issue?	_____	_____
(a) If no, go to Part II: Child's Condition.	_____	_____
2. If yes, Was there a caretaker in the home?	_____	_____
(a) What is the caretaker's relationship to the child?		
(b) If not a parent, was the caretaker there by arrangement with a parent?	_____	_____
(c) Regardless of relationship, was the caretaker able to supervise the child?	_____	_____
(d) Regardless of relationship, was the caretaker willing to supervise the child?	_____	_____
3. Did you find a caretaker who was bedridden?	_____	_____
(a) If yes, was the caretaker able to care for the child?	_____	_____
(b) If the caretaker could not care for the child, was there a neighbor or relative who was willing to provide child care?	_____	_____
4. Did you find a caretaker whose verbal or nonverbal behavior made it impossible for you to discuss the child's supervision?	_____	_____
5. Was the caretaker cooperative?	_____	_____
6. Did you find an infant alone?	_____	_____
7. Did you find a preschool age child alone?	_____	_____
8. Was the child able to care for himself? (briefly explain in the narrative)	_____	_____
9. Did you find a young child being supervised by an older sibling?	_____	_____

II. CHILD'S CONDITION

1. Was the child's condition an issue?	_____	_____
2. If no, go to Part III: Condition of the home.	_____	_____
If yes, did you observe an injured child (e.g., one with burns, lacerations, bruises, etc)?	_____	_____
(a) If yes, use the narrative section to report the caretaker's and child's explanation of how injuries were sustained.	_____	_____

3. Did you observe a child who appears to be ill? ＿＿＿＿＿＿ ＿＿＿＿＿＿
4. Did a child tell you that she or he is in pain? ＿＿＿＿＿＿ ＿＿＿＿＿＿
5. Did the child's overt behavior seem limited (e.g., the child was unable to move a limb or to turn her head)? ＿＿＿＿＿＿ ＿＿＿＿＿＿
   (a) If yes, to questions 3, 4, or 5, use the narrative section to describe what you observed or were told. ＿＿＿＿＿＿ ＿＿＿＿＿＿
6. Is there evidence to suggest that the child has received medical attention? (if yes, describe the evidence in the narrative section.) ＿＿＿＿＿＿ ＿＿＿＿＿＿
   (a) Insert the name, address, and telephone number of the medical person or clinic.

   _____

   (b) Is the caretaker's report congruent with the medical report? ＿＿＿＿＿＿ ＿＿＿＿＿＿
       (1) If no, use the narrative section to describe the discrepancy. ＿＿＿＿＿＿ ＿＿＿＿＿＿
7. Is there evidence to suggest that the caretaker has ministered to the child's medical needs? ＿＿＿＿＿＿ ＿＿＿＿＿＿
   (a) If yes, describe the evidence in the narrative. ＿＿＿＿＿＿ ＿＿＿＿＿＿

III. CONDITIONS OF THE HOME
1. Was a condition of the home an issue? ＿＿＿＿＿＿ ＿＿＿＿＿＿
   If not, go to Part IV: Protective Custody.
2. If yes, Was the outside temperature below 50 degrees F. without heat in the home? ＿＿＿＿＿＿ ＿＿＿＿＿＿
3. Were there broken windows with jagged edges of glass? ＿＿＿＿＿＿ ＿＿＿＿＿＿
4. Was there exposed electrical wiring? ＿＿＿＿＿＿ ＿＿＿＿＿＿
5. Was there indoor/outdoor bathroom facilities in working order? ＿＿＿＿＿＿ ＿＿＿＿＿＿
6. Were there rotten floorboards which would pose danger to a child? ＿＿＿＿＿＿ ＿＿＿＿＿＿
7. Were there holes in the roof through which rain or snow could enter the home? ＿＿＿＿＿＿ ＿＿＿＿＿＿
8. Was there garbage/feces in the home which you think pose a health hazard? ＿＿＿＿＿＿ ＿＿＿＿＿＿
9. Were there rats in the home? ＿＿＿＿＿＿ ＿＿＿＿＿＿
10. *OTHER:* Were there any issues not covered in Parts I through III which, in your opinion, pose danger to a child? If yes, use the narrative section to describe the condition and your reason for presuming danger. ＿＿＿＿＿＿ ＿＿＿＿＿＿

IV. Did You Take Protective Custody of a Child?

                                                    YES   NO

If yes, check which of the following reasons apply. If more than one reason is applicable, please rank the reasons in order of their importance by inserting number 1 in the space next to the most important reason, number 2 in the space next to the second reason, and so forth.

1. No caretaker able to care for child. _____
2. No caretaker willing to care for child. _____
3. Caretaker unable to care for child and no relatives or neighbors available to help. _____
4. Caretaker would not accept help. _____
5. Emergency services (e.g., homemaker, emergency caretaker) not available. _____
6. Child abandoned. _____
7. Child unable to care for self. _____
8. Child injured; caretaker would not explain how injury occurred. _____
9. Location or type of injury suggests abuse and parent's explanation is discrepant with observations. _____
10. Child's explanation is discrepant with caretaker's explanation. _____
11. Child said that she/he is afraid to stay at home. _____
12. Child appears to be seriously ill and parent will not arrange for medical examination or will not allow you to arrange for an examination. _____
13. Medical evidence of prior injuries where the location or type of injury suggests abuse. _____
14. Medical evidence of prior injuries which did not receive medical attention and medical opinion is that the injuries could not have been sustained by accident. _____
15. The type of location of the injury (burns on an infant's buttocks, whipmarks) suggest an intention to harm the child. _____
16. Home unsafe, relocation of family not possible and immediate repairs cannot be made. _____
17. Other (use narrative section to describe other reasons for taking protective custody).

NARRATIVE

selves with the statutes of the state in which they practice. The conditions that constitute abuse or neglect differ across jurisdictions. Equally important is learning about the kinds of evidence required to substantiate an allegation of maltreatment. In the state of Illinois, for example, psychological and/or psychiatric reports are needed to support charges of emotional abuse or neglect. Medical reports are required whenever physical abuse or nutritional neglect are issues.

Sources of Information

Sources of information that contribute to decision making are listed in figure 4-6. The process workers follow in reaching a determination of credible evidence and whether to open a case for services is depicted in figures 4-7.

Information from a variety of sources may contribute to decision making as should be clear from a review of data sources listed in figure 4-6. Equally clear is that allegations of maltreatment or the suggestion that a child is at risk carry the implication that parents intended to harm a child or that they refused to correct conditions creating risk whether through use of their own resources or by utilizing the resources of social agencies.

When credible evidence is provided by a reporter the basic goal of the investigation is met. The information given to the reception worker is logged in the central registry. A protective service worker will visit the family, inform them of the report, describe the evidence, explain the law, and review the implications of the report for the family. In most states, a minimum implication is that the family will have to accept services in order to reduce the likelihood of future maltreatment. In some jurisdictions, criminal charges may be filed if, for example, there is evidence of sexual abuse or if physical abuse was life-threatening. A child may be taken into protective custody or emergency services sent into the home if any of the dangerous conditions reviewed in the guidelines for an immediate home visit are found.

The information provided by a reporter coupled with the information that workers gather during a visit to the family home may be inconclusive, causing the case to be continued for further investigation. The course of the ongoing investigation will be governed by the nature of the report, the worker's observations, information elicited from family members and collateral resources, and information contained in agency archives. Before we discuss this process, let us look at the kinds of evidence staff may compile.

Real evidence consists of documents and photographs such as x rays, pictures showing a child's injuries, certified school records showing patterns of attendance, and return receipts from letters sent by registered mail.

FIGURE 4-6. Sources of Information for Determining Whether There Is Credible Evidence of Abuse or Neglect

A determination of credible evidence may be made using information:
(1) *Provided by a Reporter:* Credible evidence may exist at the time a report is made. For example, a medical person may have evidence that a child has been injured and medical opinion may hold that the injury could not have been sustained by accident.

-or-

A reporter may have observed a child being beaten and may be willing to testify to that effect.
(2) *Provided by a Parent* who acknowledges an act of abuse or neglect.
(3) Provided by a Child who states that she or he was beaten or who reports some form of sexual abuse or molestation.
(4) Provided by Psychiatric or Psychological Consultants who have tested a child and whose opinion it is that the child is suffering from emotional problems or is at risk of such problems, *and* the parent rejects the child and/or refuses assistance when offered.
(5) Provided by School Personnel whose records show repeated absences *and* there is evidence that the parent is deliberately keeping the child from attending school.
(6) Credible Evidence May Come From Worker Observations. One may observe a parent who is not able to care for a child and the parent may refuse to accept help. Consequently, the child may be taken into protective custody. A description of worker observations and parental responses may be sufficient to sustain an allegation of maltreatment.

-or-

(a) Information provided by a reporter coupled with that gained during an interview with parents and others may support allegations of maltreatment. Discrepancies between a parent and a child's explanation of how an injury was sustained, between a parent's report and medical evidence or disparities between information provided by parents and the type or location of an injury may permit inferences of how the injury was sustained.

-or-

(b) Worker observations coupled with prior information may yield credible evidence. If one finds an unsupervised child, even though immediate danger does not exist, the fact that there are prior confirmed reports, similar in nature to the report under investigation, may be sufficient to sustain an allegation of supervisorial neglect.
(7) The Available Information May Suggest But Not Confirm That Abuse Or Neglect Has Occurred. Whether there is evidence to support an allegation may not be ascertainable without continuing the investigation and gathering detailed information from parents, children and others who have pertinent data. Workers often request assistance from others, medical or psychological consultants, for instance, before a final determination. For example, observations of a child's behavior may suggest internal injuries. This directs the worker to arrange for a medical examination. Or, the child's behavior may seem so inappropriate as to suggest the need for a psychological evaluation. Should this occur, diagnostic assistance must be arranged. A final determination must await the diagnostic report.

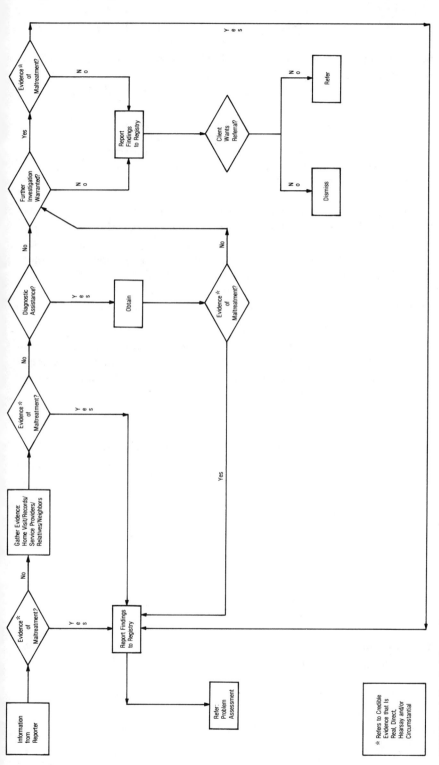

FIGURE 4-7. Is There Credible Evidence of Abuse or Neglect?

Direct evidence   comes from firsthand knowledge of events. It takes the form of statements describing what an observer saw, heard, said, and did. The following narrative recorded by a protective service worker is illustrative:

> I arrived at the Mitchell home at 7:00 A.M. The front door was ajar. I heard a child crying from inside the apartment. I knocked on the door and called out "Is anyone home?" but received no answer. I entered the apartment and found a young boy (Timothy, age 4) sitting in a corner of the living room. There was no adult in the home.

In some cases, the only evidence available comes from lay reporters who observed a child being beaten or who overheard a caretaker threaten a youngster. Information elicited from reporters should be put in writing using the informant's own words. Since facts may be distorted by time, information should be recorded at the earliest possible moment. Workers should endeavor to have lay persons give depositions, which is testimony taken under oath, for use in court.

Hearsay evidence   is secondhand information. The statement "Mrs. Smith told me that she heard Mr. Williams threaten his son," is an example. Hearsay evidence is generally not admissible in court because its accuracy cannot be ascertained through cross-examination. If possible, the worker would try to obtain firsthand evidence from Mrs. Smith.

Circumstantial evidence   is indirect proof of facts. For example, if medical opinion holds that a child's injuries could not have been sustained by accident and if we have knowledge of who was taking care of the child at the time the injury occurred, assuming that there was only one caretaker, we would infer that the person was responsible for the injuries. Circumstantial evidence plays a significant role in establishing the basis for action in protective service cases since direct proof of facts is often not available.

Using Information to Determine Whether There Is Credible Evidence of Abuse or Neglect

Many, perhaps a majority, of the cases that come to the attention of protective services are grey-area cases in which there is no real or direct evidence of maltreatment or risk to a child.

Absent such evidence, workers must create a data base using their observations, information supplied by others and that which is found in agency archives to formulate *risk hypotheses.* A risk hypothesis contains information describing the situation in which a child was found (whether the child was being supervised, for example), the condition of the child or of the child's home. And, they include evidence suggestive of parental culpability which is defined as an intention to cause harm and/or an unwillingness to take action to reduce risk that is imminent.

The information reported in risk hypotheses is one way of showing worker efforts to strike a balance between a child's right to be protected from injury and the right of parents to raise their children free from outside intervention. Evidence of parental culpability tips the scales in favor of the child and his or her right to be safeguarded from harm; hence, justifying action by protective services.

The efforts workers undertake to create this balance should be clear from a review of the guidelines for determining whether a child is in immediate danger. Questions focusing on parental actions and intentions appear throughout. To illustrate this issue, consider the first section which deals with supervision. Lack of supervision forms the basis for many of the reports made to protective services. However, save for extreme cases where a parent's inability to care for a child is beyond question or where an infant has been left unattended and a parent cannot be immediately located, determining what action to take is often difficult. Efforts to establish criteria for determining whether a child is safe that are based solely on the child's age, on the time of day the child is left alone, or the length of time the child is alone are arbitrary. This is why we focus attention on whether parents left instructions for their children, whether the child understands the instructions (e.g., knows what to do should she need help), and on whether the child is able to act on her own behalf.

We are not suggesting that parental decisions to leave children alone are necessarily correct decisions. What we are suggesting is that it would be an error to infer neglect if the parent's decision rested on his assessment of his child's ability to care for himself. When one encounters situations where parents acted according to their best judgment but where, in the worker's judgment, the actions taken place a child at risk, the worker's major task is educational. Here, the basis for assuming risk is described to parents and ways of reducing risk are explored (engaging a child care person, enrolling a youngster in day care, or teaching a child self-help skills). If a parent will not act to reduce risk, will not accept agency services or if there are prior reports similar in nature to the report under investigation, a basis for protective service action can be established. Some examples of how workers document risk are as follows:

John Smith (age 6) is left unsupervised each day between 2 P.M. when school ends, and 6 P.M. when his mother returns from work. There is no telephone in the home nor are there neighbors within walking distance to whom the child can turn for help. John's mother, Mrs. Alicia Smith, refuses to enroll John in day care and will not engage a child care person nor will she permit this worker to make arrangements for child care.

Steven and Richard Hite (age 4 and 5, respectively) are left in the care of their elder sister, Michelle (age 14), each weekday evening from 7 P.M. until 2 A.M. while their mother, Stephanie Hite, is at work. Michelle Hite told this worker that she "sometimes goes out with friends," leaving the children to care for themselves. Mrs. Hite stated that she sees "nothing wrong with this situation" and that she will not "spend good money on a babysitter."

Andrew Felix, father of Timothy and Jane Felix, twins (age 5), denies leaving his children unsupervised. There are two prior reports on the Felix family. Agency records show that Mr. Felix agreed to enroll his children in day care subsequent to the last report. Records of the Hillside Day Care Center show that Mr. Felix inquired into their program but did not follow up on his inquiry. Mr. Felix states that he chose to supervise his children himself rather than enroll them in day care. Since this is the third report it seems advisable to open this case to ensure that child care arrangements are made and followed through.

It is important to bear in mind that some of our concerns about a child's safety are generated more by differences between our own child-rearing practices and those of others than they are by any evidence of imminent danger. Developing risk hypotheses according to the guidelines presented here is one way of reducing the chances that value judgments will exert an undue influence on decision making.

Some of the conditions that workers observe are caused by knowledge, skill, and income deficits. A parent may not know what constitutes a well-balanced diet, may not know how to access community resources when help is needed, may lack skills in caring for a newborn or be unable to afford child care services or home repairs. Here, too, it would not be reasonable to allege maltreatment unless the parent refused help when offered.

Certain types of allegations cannot be upheld without information from third parties. Whether a child is suffering from malnutrition is a medical determination. Charges of educational neglect generally require documentation from school authorities showing the frequency of a child's absences. Diagnostic assistance may be required because a worker has not been trained in certain assessment procedures. Several examples follow showing how information from third parties is used to determine whether there is evidence to sustain charges of maltreatment.

Example 1   The Rodriguez family came to the attention of protective services following a report by a school social worker that Anita Rodriguez (age 14) had been truant from school several days each month for a three-month period of time. School records showed that the school social worker had made repeated efforts to meet with the young girl's mother. Included here were seven attempts to reach Mrs. Rodriguez by telephone (none of the calls were returned) and three letters sent to the mother describing Anita's truancy and requesting that Mrs. Rodriguez contact the school to set up an appointment to discuss the issue of Anita's absences. The letters were never answered. Two of the letters had been sent by registered mail; the return receipts indicated that the mother had received them.

Mrs. Rodriguez was no more cooperative with the protective service worker than she had been with the school social worker. Here, the key to supporting an allegation of educational neglect was the mother's tacit acceptance of her daughter's behavior, evidenced by her unwillingness to meet with school authorities. If Mrs. Rodriguez had been cooperative, this case would not have been opened to protective services on the basis of educational neglect. The mother's seeming lack of interest is required as evidence to support a petition of educational neglect. Without the documentation provided by the school social worker the charges would not have been upheld in court.

Example 2   A protective service worker observed bruises on a youngster's face and arms which the parent explained by saying that the child had fallen off of her bicycle. The child confirmed the report. The worker arranged for the youngster to be examined by a physician who subsequently reported that the location and type of injury could not have been sustained in the manner suggested. The discrepancy between the report of the parent and that of the physician is the key issue. The task that confronted the worker was to inform the parent of this discrepancy and to request a factual account of how the injuries were sustained.

The disparity between the report made by parent and child and that made by the physician is not proof of parental culpability. But, unless a satisfactory explanation is offered, the lack of congruence would be a sufficient basis for hypothesizing that the parent caused the injury or was aware of who had caused it and was not willing to divulge this information. In fact, the youngster's injuries were caused by the parent who lost control while disciplining the child.

Example 3   During a home visit a worker observed a youngster sitting in a chair in the corner of a room. The child would not, when asked, sit by the worker and his parent. His response to questions was hesitant and his affect flat, e.g., his voice was monotonic and he did not look at the person to whom he was speaking.

The child's behavior could be caused by nervousness in the interview situation, it could be indicative of behavioral norms of a subculture different from that of the worker, or it could be reflective of a more generalized problem. To confirm which hypothesis was correct the worker sought information from different sources. She contacted the youngster's school, inquiring about his behavior in and outside of the classroom, she queried relatives and friends of the family and arranged to observe the child at school, at play, and interacting with his parents. The worker also arranged for psychological testing. Additional information indicated that the behaviors observed during the initial interview were representative of the child's behavior elsewhere and that they were not normative for his peer group. Thus, the suggestion that help was needed was a reasonable one.

The course of action that workers follow in situations such as this depends upon parental response to the suggestion that help is necessary. If a parent accepts the suggestion that help is needed (and assuming that the parent has not previously withdrawn from a program designed to assist the family with this difficulty), services could be provided on a voluntary basis. The parent's willingness to accept assistance would not support an hypothesis that the parent's behavior was creating risk for the child. Whether service was offered by the protective agency or the client referred elsewhere would depend upon worker skill-level, worker time to provide direct problem-solving services, and the availability of community programs to provide help.

If assistance is offered and refused, or if the client's service history raises doubts as to the likelihood of continuing with services on a voluntary basis, there would be sufficient grounds for proceeding on involuntary grounds. A refusal of help in the face of evidence that it is needed would support an hypothesis that the parent's concern for the youngster, expressed in the refusal of help, is less than what we would expect of parents in our society, thus falling below minimum expectations.

There are situations in which a parent's behavior has not had an observable effect on a child but where risk may exist. Parental expectations may be inappropriate to the child's age. For instance, a three-year-old may be expected to eat all of the food on her plate, not to make a mess, and to pick up and put away all of her toys each time she finishes playing with them. The parent may report feeling extremely frustrated by the child's inability to live up to his expectations and may state that he cannot understand why his child is different from other three-year-olds. When asked how he deals with his frustration, the client may note that he does not know what to do but feels as though he might "explode."

The child cannot meet her father's expectations due to her age. The father's frustration level is high and his statement that he does not know how to deal with his feelings lends credibility to the suggestion that the child is in danger even though she has not been injured. The child may never be injured. The point, however, is that the facts would lead a reasonable person to conclude that the possibility of risk exists and that intervention to reduce risk is warranted.

Risk hypotheses become less tenable as one moves away from the facts. An unreasonable hypothesis is usually replete with inferences and not supported by evidence. Often such hypotheses focus on long-range effects such as the suggestion that a child whose parents are undergoing divorce will, ipso facto, suffer emotionally in the long run.

When there is no evidence of abuse or neglect nor a basis for inferring risk, clients are referred for services if they want assistance with problems that fall outside of the purview of protective services. The facts garnered during the investigation are reported to the state central registry.

A Note on Risk Taking   Deciding whether to open a case to protective services and decisions whether to leave children in the care of their parents involve an element of risk taking since one cannot predict the course of events that will follow a home visit.

The only way to ensure a child's safety is to remove the youngster or to send a live-in caretaker into the home. Removing all of the children who are the subject of protective service reports as a way of reducing risk is a practical impossibility and one that would not be socially acceptable. Removal of children constitutes an extreme example of invasion of family privacy. Live-in caretakers may reduce risk temporarily, but eventually one must confront leaving children alone with their parents. There are no sure ways of eliminating risk.

An example will illustrate the dilemma confronting workers. Responding to a report of supervisorial neglect, Jeanne Carlysle visited the Damien home. Mrs. Damien was present. She denied having left her 4-year-old son, William, unattended. The mother was a full-time homemaker who said that she either took her son with her when she left home or that she engaged a babysitter whose name and telephone number she gave to the worker. The babysitter confirmed working for Mrs. Damien on occasion. There were no prior reports and no basis for further action. Twenty-four hours after the investigation a fire broke out in the Damien home. William died of smoke inhalation. Mrs. Damien was not at home when the tragedy occurred.

Fortunately, a case such as this is exceptional. It does, however, illustrate a dilemma of protective service work. Workers are interested in processes or patterns of child care that occur over time. However, process information is difficult to obtain and is rarely available when initial decisions with critical implications for a child's safety are made. Patterns of child care may be established if prior reports exist or if services were provided and client behavior rigorously documented.

The facts gathered by the worker in the Damien case would not have supported any course of action other than the one taken by the worker. Clearly, Mrs. Damien's behavior 24 hours after the visit could not have been predicted.

Notes and References

1. Adopted, in part, from Theodore J. Stein and Tina L. Rzepnicki, "Decision Making in Child Welfare: Current Issues and Future Directions," in *Child Welfare: Current Dilemmas— Future Directions*, eds. Brenda G. McGowan and William Meezan (Itasca, Illinois: F. E. Peacock Publishers, 1983), pp. 259–294.

2. Technology that is available to help familiies with problem resolution is a major variable in the professional domain. Current technology is limited as are resources such as day care and homemakers. See Cecelia E. Sudia, "What Services do Abusing and Neglecting Families Need?" in *The Social Context of Child Abuse and Neglect,* ed. Leroy H. Pelton (New York: Human Sciences Press, Inc., 1981), ch. 9; Stephen Magura, "Are Services to Prevent Foster Care Effective?" *Children and Youth Services Review,* Vol. 3, No. 3 (1981), pp. 193–212.

3. See Robert H. Mnookin, "Child Custody Adjudication: Judicial Function in the Face of Indeterminancy," *Law and Contemporary Problems,* Vol. 39 (Summer 1975), pp. 226–293; Institute of Judicial Administration, American Bar Association, Juvenile Justice Standards Project, *Standards Relating to Abuse and Neglect: Tentative Draft* (Cambridge, Mass.: Ballinger Publishing Co., 1977); Joseph Goldstein, Anna Freud, and Albert J. Solnit, *Beyond the Best Interests of the Child* (New York: The Free Press, 1973); Joseph Goldstein, Anna Freud, and Albert J. Solnit, *Before the Best Interests of the Child* (New York: The Free Press, 1979).

Much of the criticism of the best interest standard centers on situations where intervention is coercive; where court action is evoked because parents will not accept services on a voluntary basis. Voluntary requests for assistance may not, initially, involve court action. Criticisms that center on violations of family privacy are not usually viewed as applicable when services are voluntarily requested. Unlike situations where intervention proceeds on the basis of court assumption of jurisdiction over a child, voluntary clients may, in theory, withdraw from services at any time.

Our position is that a revised standard for decision making is as pertinent to voluntary as it is to involuntary cases. First, practitioners and judges need guidelines for decision making and these are, at present, derived from the best interest standard. Thus, families may be evaluated against an ideal which, in turn, may result in setting unrealistic expectations for family functioning. This may result in an evaluation of family inadequacy and lead to court intervention when voluntary parents decide to withdraw from services. We know that many children in out-of-home placement entered care via voluntary requests for service. (See: Alan R. Gruber, *Children in Foster Care: Destitute, Neglected . . . . Betrayed* (New York: Human Sciences Press, 1978), p. 37.) Once in a substitute placement, parents are at risk of having their behavior evaluated using the best interest test and of finding, when they ask to have their children returned, that court action is taken.

4. Walter Barnett, *Sexual Freedom and the Constitution: An Inquiry into the Constitutionality of Repressive Sex Laws* (Albuquerque, New Mexico: University of New Mexico Press, 1973), p.21.

5. Bernice Boehm, "An Assessment of Family Adequacy in Protective Cases," Child Welfare, Vol. 41 (January 1962), pp. 10–16.

6. Grounds for determining neglect, which include conditions such as "home is an unfit place, lack of proper parental care, control or guardianship, and moral unfitness of parent," are sufficiently broad to encompass the behaviors involved in substance abuse. See Stanford N. Katz, Ruth-Arlene Howe, and Melba McGrath, "Child Neglect Laws in America," Family Law Quarterly, Vol. IX, No. 1 (Spring 1975), pp. 25–27.

7. Jeanne M. Giovannoni and Rosina M. Becerra, *Defining Child Abuse* (New York: The Free Press, 1979), p. 235.

8. David Fanshel and Eugene B. Shinn, *Children in Foster Care: A Longitudinal Investigation* (New York: Columbia University Press, 1978), ch. 4.

9. Kermit T. Wiltse, "Current Issues and New Directions in Foster Care," in *Child Welfare Strategies in the Coming Years* (Washington, D.C.: U.S. Department of Health, Education and Welfare, DHEW Publication No. (OHDS) 78-30158, 1978), p. 61.

10. Theodore J. Stein, Eileen D. Gambrill, and Kermit T. Wiltse, *Children in Foster Homes: Achieving Continuity in Care* (New York: Praeger Publishers, 1978), pp. 86–87, 113.

11. Ann W. Shyne and Anita G. Schroeder, *National Study of Social Services to Children and Their Families* (Washington, D.C.: United States Children's Bureau, DHEW Publication No. (OHDS) 78-30150, 1978), p. 77.

12. Clinical decisions are those that often require some measure of worker judgment in selecting a final option. Decisions involving client eligibility for cash and in-kind services, where a predefined set of criteria are applied to a known set of client characteristics, were not considered.

13. An emergency response is one requiring immediate action. The worker does not have the 24-hour response time permitted by state law.

14. The following material is taken from Theodore J. Stein and Tina L. Rzepnicki, *Decision Making at Child Welfare Intake—A Handbook for Practitioners* (New York: Child Welfare League of America, 1983).

15. Occasionally the child may not be in a home when an emergency visit is required, in which case the worker would go to wherever the child is located. This might happen, for instance, when the school makes a report that a child is afraid to go home.

16. For an overview of the conditions that constitute child abuse and neglect in each of the states, see *Trends in Child Protection Laws—1979* (Denver, Colorado: Education Commission of the States, October 1979).

17. If a parent is not cooperative, but the child is being supervised and her physical condition and conditions of the home do not suggest a problem, there are probably no reasonable grounds for further action.

5 DESCRIPTION OF THE ILLINOIS/WEST VIRGINIA PROJECT

The Illinois/West Virginia Project was a three-year research and demonstration effort funded by the United States Children's Bureau. Its main purpose was to develop and test procedures for decision making at child welfare intake.[1] Intake was defined to include all transactions that occur between workers and clients from the point of initial contact through development of a service plan.[2]

Project Implementation: The Field Test Sites

The field test was conducted in three child welfare agencies in two states. The Illinois Department of Children and Family Services and West Virginia's Department of Welfare represented the public sector; Catholic Charities of Chicago, the private sector. The populations served by these agencies and characteristics of the setting are described below.

Illinois

Population   Two-thirds of the 11.2 million people living in the State of Illinois reside in the Chicago metropolitan area, including two-thirds of the state's children.[3] Fifty percent of the population is white, 40 percent black, and approximately 14 percent are Hispanic.[4]

Seventy-two percent of the 223,300 families receiving AFDC in Illinois live in Cook County (Chicago and adjacent suburbs). Sixty-seven percent of the recipients are black, 28 percent are white, and 5 percent are of other racial groups.[5]

Settings   The *Illinois Department of Children and Family Services* (IDCFS) is the cabinet-level agency responsible for providing social services to children and their families. The central office in Springfield is responsible for state-wide planning, policy, monitoring and evaluation, staff development, technical assistance, and other supportive services. Income maintenance programs are handled separately through the Department of Public Aid.

IDCFS is organized into eight decentralized regions.[6] Regional offices supervise the 78 field offices spread across the state. There are 13 field offices in Chicago. The Department's child welfare program serves 10,000 families with 30,000 children.

IDCFS offers a broad range of services most of which are provided through the department's purchase of services from private community-based agencies. The department retains authority over investigations for abuse and neglect, assessment and planning of cases, and the monitoring of services provided by other agencies."[7] The worker's role as decision maker and case manager is emphasized.[8] In Chicago, services are provided either through Child Protective Services (CPS) or Child Welfare Services (CWS) through which families can voluntarily access agency programs.

CPS reports are made to the state hotline in Springfield where they are logged on a computerized central registry. A check for prior reports is conducted, subseqent to which the complaint is forwarded to a regional office for investigation. All reports must be investigated within 24 hours of their receipt.

When the project began, investigative responsibilities were divided between intake units—two in each of three 8-hour shifts to provide 24-hour-a-day service—and four protective service teams which served the county by geographic subdivision.[9] The division of responsibility between intake units and teams varied. At one extreme, the intake unit would initiate contact with the reported family only, the team completing the investigation and making the determination of whether there was credible evidence of abuse or neglect.[10] At the other extreme, the intake worker would complete the investigation and forward a case to the team only if there was credible evidence of maltreatment and services were to be offered.[11] The amount of time available to workers was often the main determinant of this process. Team workers were responsible for case planning, arranging for services, and monitoring service delivery.

In June of 1979, 46 percent of the children under the supervision of IDCFS were served in their own homes while 32 percent were in foster homes and 22 percent in other substitute care arrangements.[12]

Catholic Charities of Chicago (CC) is the only private agency sanctioned to conduct protective service investigations for the IDCFS. Responsibility for case management is divided between three units. The intake unit receives referrals from the Chicago office of the IDCFS following their referral from the state hotline. Workers are responsible for determining whether there is credible evidence of abuse or neglect. If maltreatment is substantiated, cases go either to the In-Home Protective Service unit or to the Specialized Emergency Foster Care unit where problem assessment (which begins at intake) is completed and service plans are developed and implemented.

West Virginia

Population   West Virginia has a population of 1.9 million persons, two-thirds of whom live in nonmetropolitan areas. Marion County, the area served by the Fairmont office of the Department of Welfare where the field test was conducted, has 65,789 residents, 23,000 of whom reside in the town of Fairmont. The racial distribution in the county is 96 percent white, 3.4 percent black, and .7 percent Hispanic.[13] Although our study sample was drawn primarily from the Marion County office, some control cases came from Monongalia County. These two offices serve contiguous counties with similar populations.[14] Both county offices are managed by the same area administrator.

Fifteen percent of the state's population have incomes below the poverty line. Approximately 81 percent of these families live in rural areas.[15] Of the families receiving AFDC throughout the state, approximately five percent live in the area served during the field test.[16]

The West Virginia Department of Welfare (WVDOW) provides social services for individuals who are financially eligible or are members of a group which has been declared eligible for services regardless of income such as children who are available for adoption, juvenile offenders, adolescent or single parents, senior citizens, and individuals who are developmentally disabled. There are 27 area offices across the state. Area office administrators are directly responsible to administrators at the state level.

Each county office in West Virginia has a common intake for all services. A reception worker receives the report, referral, or request for assistance and channels it to the proper departmental unit. There is no central hotline as in Illinois nor was there a state-wide central registry for recording of abuse and neglect complaints at the time of the field test. As in Illinois, intake workers must make a home visit within 24 hours and all reports must be investigated. The intake worker conducts the entire investigation. Cases that are opened to the agency are referred for in-home services or foster care services.

Voluntary child welfare services are provided through the agency's Youth Services and Community Delinquency divisions which are also responsible for court-referred cases (where abuse or neglect is not alleged) and for children over whom the Department has legal custody who have been adjudicated delinquent.

The estimated number of persons served in the Marion and Monongalia offices during the 1981 fiscal year include 700 in child protective services, 240 in foster care, 120 in youth and community delinquency services, and 15 in adoptions. Overall, this represents approximately 6 percent of the persons receiving similar services across the state.[17]

The Research Hypotheses and Research Design

The hypotheses that guided our work are as follows:

(1) The use of structured decision-making procedures, in which data elements for making decisions are identified and rules for using information are offered, would increase inter-judge reliability in decision making relative to the use of a nonstructured approach to decision making.

(2) A structured approach to decision making would be more efficient than a nonstructured approach. Efficiency was defined in terms of the time workers spend in gathering and analyzing data for decision making and in consultation with supervisors, colleagues and collaterals on issues related to decision making.

(3) If a structured approach to decision making was more efficient, case plans could be formulated earlier than when the decision maker lacks a structure for selecting options.

We were also interested in whether use of a structured framework for decision making would effect recidivism (defined as second or third reports of maltreatment subsequent to completion of an investigation) and whether outcomes for children in terms of the numbers taken into protective custody or placed in foster home care would differ relative to cases managed by workers lacking a structure for decision making. These latter concerns were not formulated as hypotheses.

Cases were randomly assigned to experimental and control staff at intake by unit supervisors. Method of assignment is discussed below.

It was our intention to track cases from experimental and control intake units into the geographic teams and service units at IDCFS and Catholic

Charities. Tracking of cases was to serve a dual purpose: first, we wanted data descriptive of the decision-making processes undertaken by team and service workers that were comparable to the data we were gathering from intake staff. Monitoring the effects on the decision-making behavior of team and service workers, as a function of whether a case came from an experimental or control intake unit, was a second concern. We were not able to use the data from the geographic teams at IDCFS for the reasons discussed below.

Team workers did not want to be involved in the project. Despite requests for cooperation from project staff and from agency administrators in Springfield, worker involvement was minimal at best. Evidence of disinterest became apparent when we undertook to analyze our data.

One hundred and eleven cases were assigned to experimental workers (table 5-1); 52 to intake units (47%); 59 to experimental teams (53%). Data on the process of decision making were not reported for 34 of the 59 cases assigned to experimental teams, leaving us with a nonrandom sample of 25 cases.

A more serious problem came to our attention when we began the analysis of data for those cases where process information was provided. Process forms completed by workers asked whether they or someone else had made each decision. We calculated the average number of decisions workers made for each case by subtracting the number of decisions made by others from the number that could have been made. Workers in experimental teams averaged 3.8 decisions per case in contrast to an average for control staff of 5.9 decisions per case. (($p \leq .001$).

A random check of cases assigned to experimental and control staff showed that there were no significant differences on any case characteristic[18] such as

TABLE 5-1. Number of Families for Whom Decision-Making Data are Reported by Test Site

	IDCFS		CC		WVDOW	
	Exp.	Cont.	Exp.	Cont.	Exp.	Cont.
Families	111	81	60	60	19	15
Cases						
Omitted	59	81				
Missing Data	4		1	3		
Cases Reported*	48	0	59	57	19	15

*At the IDCFS there was a total of 99 experimental unit children, at CC there were 227 children (Exp. $n = 115$) (Cont. $n = 112$), and at WVDOW there were 43 children (Exp. $n = 26$) (Cont. $n = 17$).

the source of the report, type of maltreatment alleged, family composition, or prior service history which might explain this discrepancy.

We must assume that these data were not accurately reported. The 59 cases assigned to the experimental geographic teams were dropped from the analysis. The IDCFS cases we will report come from two intake units only. A third intake unit, which was to have been a part of the project, was not involved. Moreover, we received only seven cases from intake control units. Since these cases would constitute a biased sample, they are omitted from the analysis. Finally, data were missing on four cases. Consequently, for the IDCFS, data are reported for 48 intake unit experimental cases only. The reasons for non-participation of so many IDCFS staff are discussed in chapter 8.

The loss of data from the teams is unfortunate since these workers bear responsibility for case assessment and service planning. Hence, data on decisions made during the last phase of intake are not available from the Illinois public agency. Fortunately, we do have information regarding assessment and service planning decisions from both Catholic Charities and the West Virginia Department of Welfare.

Selection of Experimental and Control Units:

One of the two experimental intake units at the IDCFS volunteered for the project; the other was drafted by administration.[19] There were five workers in each unit. There is only one intake unit at Catholic Charities. The workers in that unit were divided into experimental (n-6) and control (n-5). Staff who were new to the agency and those with experience who wanted to test the decision-making procedures served as experimental workers. Additionally, five workers who provide in-home protective services and four who offer specialized emergency foster care served as experimental staff. There were no control workers in these units (table 5-2).

TABLE 5-2.   Number and Percentage of Workers by Test Site

	IDCFS	Site Catholic Charities	WVDOW	Total
Exp.	10 (100%)	15 (75%)	5 (63%)	30 (79%)
Cont.		5 (25%)	3 (37%)	8 (21%)
Total	10 (100%)	20 (100%)	8 (100%)	38 (100%)

In West Virginia, a reception social worker bore responsibility for accepting referrals, for determining whether there was a time-critical need based on the content of the request or complaint, and for sending the referral to the appropriate unit supervisor. This person served as an experimental worker. Back-up staff who occasionally performed the reception function served as control.

In the Marion County office there were two child protective teams with three members; one each responsible for intake, long-term services to families in their own homes, and foster care services. One team was chosen by administration to serve as the experimental unit; the other as control. The unit with the lowest staff turnover was chosen to act as the experimental unit.

Worker Characteristics

IDCFS   Ten protective service workers participated in the project (table 5-2). The median age of workers was 33 years (range-26 to 45); 70 percent (n-7) were male and 30 percent (n-3) were female. All held college degrees, one of which was a Bachelor of Social Work degree; eight held bachelor's degrees in related fields such as psychology or sociology, and one person held a master's degree in the humanities. Eight of the workers had more than two years of experience in child welfare preceding implementation of the project; two had more than five years of experience. There was no staff turnover during the project.

Catholic Charities   Fifteen workers (75%) served as experimental staff; five (25%) as control (table 5-2). Eighty percent (n-16) were female and 20 percent (n-4) were male. The age range was 22 to 40 years (median-30). All of the workers were college graduates. Half held a bachelor's degree, half a master's degree. Eighty-five percent (n-17) held degrees in social work or a related area. Overall, these individuals reported less experience in child welfare than did workers at IDCFS. Seventy percent (n-14) had more than one year of child welfare experience when the project began. Slightly more than half of the workers (60%/n-12) had been in their current position from one month to one year. One worker left the agency during the project.

West Virginia Department of Welfare   Eight workers, seven women and one man, serving Marion and Monongalia counties, carried experimental and control cases (table 5-2).

The age range of the workers was 24 to 45 years with a median age of 32. All staff members held college degrees, 75 percent of which were in social work or a related field. Sixty-three percent had a bachelor's degree (n-5), 25 percent (n-2) a master's degree, with one person holding an Associate of Arts degree. All of the workers had two or more years of experience in child welfare. During the field test, one worker who was involved in the project left the agency.

The Selection of Cases

Cases were randomly assigned by supervisors at all test sites.[20] At both the IDCFS and Catholic Charities ten cases each month were randomly assigned to intake workers. At Catholic Charities all of these cases continued as experimental cases when transferred to service units. Workers at the West Virginia Department of Welfare agreed to handle a maximum of four project cases at any one time.

The procedure for assigning cases was as follows. At IDCFS intake the first three cases received during the first and third weeks of each month and the first two cases received during the second and fourth weeks were included in our sample. Cases were assigned to workers on a rotating basis so that worker number one received the first case assigned, worker number two the second case, and so forth. Assignment by rotation was used at all test sites in all units. At Catholic Charities assignment began with the first case received each month subsequent to which the third, fifth, seventh, etc., cases became project cases up to the maximum number of cases workers had agreed to carry. In West Virginia a case was designated as experimental or control if the worker to whom it was assigned was carrying fewer than the agreed-upon four project cases. Otherwise, the case became a part of the workers nonproject caseload.

Case Characteristics

The clients who participated in the project are described and characteristics of the referrals are reported in the following pages. All data reported in this section were gathered by a member of the research staff. Therefore, we have descriptive information on all IDCFS cases assigned to the project against which we were able to compare the nonrandom subsample of 48 cases which forms the basis for analysis of the IDCFS data reported in chapters 6 and 7. Unless otherwise noted, the subsample is representative of the universe of cases assigned to the project.

Case Status at Time of Referral

The greatest percentage of cases referred to the project were new[21] (table 5-3), representing between 71 percent of those in West Virginia control to 89 percent in Catholic Charities control. Eighteen percent of the cases in West Virginia were reopened to the agency (twice the percentage for both Illinois sites). Eight percent of the cases at IDCFS and nine percent in West Virginia were already active at the time an occurrence of maltreatment was reported, in contrast to three percent at Catholic Charities. There were no significant differences in case status between experimental and control units at Catholic Charities and West Virginia nor were there any significant differences across sites.

Method of Referral

All protective service reports in Illinois are telephoned into the central hotline in Springfield. In West Virginia the majority of reports (82%) were phoned in directly to the agency, 12 percent were walk-ins, and 6 percent were received through the mail. There were no significant differences between experimental and control groups in West Virginia.

Source of Referral

In Illinois, medical personnel account for the greatest percentage of reports from any single source for public agency cases (29%/table 5-4). By contrast, parents or relatives were the main source of reports for Catholic Charities cases (25%) and for those in West Virginia. Reports from nonprofessionals (parent/

TABLE 5-3. Percentage of Experimental and Control Families by Case Status at Time of Referral to Project

				Site			
	IDCFS		*CC*			*WVDOW*	
Status	*Exp.*	*Exp.*	*Cont.*	*Total*	*Exp.*	*Cont.*	*Total*
	(n = 48)	(n = 59)	(n = 57)	(n = 116)	(n = 19)	(n = 15)	(n = 34)
New	82%	87%	89%	88%	74%	71%	73%
Reopen	9%	10%	8%	9%	16%	21%	18%
Active	8%	3%	3%	3%	11%	7%	9%

relative or friend/neighbor/acquaintance) taken together, were the source of almost half of all Catholic Charities cases (45%) and those in West Virginia, where they comprised 47 percent of reporting sources. These sources accounted for 40 percent of the cases at the IDCFS. Six percent of the reports made in West Virginia were from medical personnel while at Catholic Charities they were the third most important source of reports (19%).

While not reaching statistical significance, there was a difference in reporting sources between IDCFS cases included here and the universe of those assigned to the project. A greater percentage of the total sample was reported by school personnel and social service personnel (27% compared to 19% for the subsample) with 19 percent of all reports coming from parents/relatives or friends/neighbors/acquaintances compared to 40 percent of those shown in table 5-4. This is due to the fact that the intake units who carried the 48 cases on which we are reporting worked the evening and midnight shifts (4 P.M. to 8 A.M., inclusively) when school and social service professionals are least likely to be working.

School and day care staff account for 21 percent of the reports made in West Virginia and 3 percent of those served by Catholic Charities. Legal authorities account for a small percentage of IDCFS reports (4%) compared to Catholic Charities (11%) and West Virginia (12%). Finally, reports made by others accounted for 14 percent of the cases at Catholic Charities, 8 percent at the IDCFS, and 6 percent at the West Virginia Department of Welfare.

The difference in reporting sources between IDCFS and Catholic Charities is due to the fact that the greatest percentage of cases referred to the voluntary agency are neglect reports (78% compared to 48% of the reports handled by IDCFS staff/$p \leq .05$/table 5-5).[22]

Reason for Referral

The mean number of allegations per case was 1.7 for IDCFS, 1.6 for Catholic Charities, and 1.3 for the West Virginia Department of Welfare. In the public agencies, the percentage of cases where abuse and neglect were alleged was almost the same in Illinois (abuse, 52%; neglect, 48%) and equal in West Virginia (table 5-5). This is in marked contrast to Catholic Charities where 78 percent of the allegations were for neglect, only 22 percent for abuse. The only significant difference in the data shown in table 5-5 was between the total number of abuse compared to neglect cases handled by Catholic Charities relative to IDCFS and West Virginia ($p \leq .001$).

Regardless of the test site, burns, wounds, cuts, bruises, and welts were the most commonly reported injuries, followed by other abuse.[23] Together, these

TABLE 5-4. Percentage of Experimental and Control Families by Source of Referral

			Site				
	IDCFS	CC			WVDOW		
Referral Source	Exp.	Exp.	Cont.	Total	Exp.	Cont.	Total
	(n = 40)[e]	(n = 59)	(n = 57)	(n = 116)	(n = 19)	(n = 15)	(n = 34)
Medical Personnel[a]	29%	23%	15%	19%	5%	7%	6%
Legal Authorities[b]	4%	5%	16%	11%	5%	20%	12%
Social Services[c]	2%	12%	5%	8%	11%	7%	9%
School/Day Care	17%	5%	2%	3%	21%	20%	21%
Parent/Relative	19%	27%	24%	25%	42%	13%	29%
Friend/Neighbor Acquaintance	21%	13%	26%	20%	11%	27%	18%
Other[d]	8%	15%	13%	14%	5%	7%	6%

[a] Physicians, nurses, hospital social workers; [b] police, court, other legal personnel; [c] state, city social service personnel, in-house referrals, private social service agencies; [d] victim, anonymous, other sources not specified. [e] Data was missing on 8 IDCFS cases.

The only significant difference is between IDCFS and CC totals (WV cell frequencies are too small for a test of significance) Chi-square = 13.74 (6 degrees of freedom) $p \leq .05$.

TABLE 5-5. Percentage of Each Type of Allegation for Experimental and Control Children[a]

Allegation	IDCFS	CC			WVDOW		
	Exp.	Exp.	Cont.	Total	Exp.	Cont.	Total
	(n = 66)	(n = 97)	(n = 106)	(n = 203)	(n = 23)	(n = 21)	(n = 44)
ABUSE							
burns, wounds, cuts, bruises, welts	47%	55%	55%	55%	50%	20%	36%
excessive corporal punishment and torture	11%	5%	14%	9%		40%	18%
sexual abuse[b]	6%				25%		14%
other abuse[c]	35%	41%	32%	36%	25%	40%	32%
TOTAL ABUSE	34 (52%)	22 (24%)	22 (21%)	44 (22%)	12 (52%)	10 (48%)	22 (50%)
NEGLECT							
Supervision:							
Caretaker present	19%	21%	18%	19%	9%	45%	27%
No caretaker/abandonment	31%	33%	36%	35%	9%		5%
Inadequate food, clothing, shelter	16%	19%	23%	22%	27%	27%	27%
Medical neglect[d]	16%	5%	6%	6%	36%	18%	27%
Other neglect[e]	19%	21%	18%	18%	18%	9%	14%
TOTAL NEGLECT	32 (48%)	75 (76%)	84 (79%)	159 (78%)	11 (48%)	11 (52%)	22 (50%)

[a] Number of allegations exceeds number of cases because of multiple allegations in some cases. Percentages reflect totals of abuse or neglect; [b] sexual intercourse, molestation, exploitation; [c] death, bites, tying up, or close confinement, drug/alcohol abuse, and other, nonspecified abuse; [d] includes malnutrition, failure to thrive, and venereal disease; [e] educational neglect and other, nonspecified neglect. The only significant difference in these data are between totals of abuse and neglect across 3 sites. Chi-square = 38.26 (2 degrees of freedom) $p \leq .001$.

categories account for between 60 percent and 96 percent of reported injuries. The greatest percentage of neglect reports in any one category for Illinois cases involves the absence of a caretaker (IDCFS:31%; CC:35%). In fact, nonsupervision whether or not a caretaker was present accounts for half of all neglect reports in Illinois.

In West Virginia, 27 percent of neglect reports involve nonsupervision with a caretaker present. Equal percentages of neglect reports involve allegations of inadequate food, clothing, and shelter or medical neglect. These latter categories, taken together, account for 32 percent of the cases investigated by IDCFS and 28 percent of those investigated by Catholic Charities. Reports of miscellaneous types of neglect are approximately equal across the three sites, accounting for 14 percent in West Virginia to 21 percent of reports at Catholic Charities.

Family Characteristics

Family Composition   The majority of families were headed by single parents, although the overall percentage of two-parent families was somewhat greater in West Virginia than in Illinois (48% for West Virginia compared to 31% and 24% for IDCFS and Catholic Charities, respectively; table 5-6). The difference in family composition between both Illinois sites and West Virginia is significant ($p = \leq .01$).

Regardless of the test site or the service, over 90 percent of all single-parent families were female headed.

Ages of Parents and Children   The women who headed families receiving services through the project ranged in age from 20 to 29 years. Males were between the ages of 30 and 39 years.

At both public agencies, the greatest percentage of children was found in the over-13 age category: (IDCFS: 26%; W.V.: 35%/table 5-7). Children age 1 year to 3 years account for the greatest percentage in any single age category at the voluntary agency (30%) where only seven percent of youngsters were 13 years of age or older. Overall, children 6 years of age or younger constitute the majority of the Catholic Charities sample (66%) and approximately one-half of the sample at the IDCFS (47%) and in West Virginia (51%). The only significant difference in these data is in comparison of totals across the three sites ($p \leq .001$).

Ethnicity   Approximately 35 percent of the Illinois sample were white compared to 88 percent of those in West Virginia. Black parents comprised 51

TABLE 5-6. Percentage of Experimental and Control Families by Family Composition

| | | | | | Site | | | | |
| | IDCFS[a] | | CC | | | | WVDOW | | |
Family Composition	Exp.	Cont.	Exp.	Cont.	Total		Exp.	Cont.	Total
	(n=41)	(n=59)	(n=56)	(n=115)			(n=19)	(n=13)	(n=32)
Single	67%	70%	79%	74%			47%	57%	52%
2-parent[b]	31%	27%	21%	24%			53%	43%	48%
Other[c]	2%	3%		2%					

[a] Data were missing on 7 IDCFS cases, on 1 CC control case, and on 2 control cases from the WVDOW; [b] includes parent living with unrelated adult; [c] unidentified. The only significant difference in these data is for totals across 3 sites. Chi-square = 12.6 (2 degrees of freedom) $p \leq .01$ (Other category omitted.)

TABLE 5-7. Age Distribution of Experimental and Control Children

			Site				
	IDCFS		CC^a			*WVDOW*	
Age	*Exp.*	*Exp.*	*Cont.*	*Total*	*Exp.*	*Cont.*	*Total*
	($n=99$)	($n=115$)	($n=111$)	($n=226$)	($n=26$)	($n=16$)	($n=42$)
<1	12%	15%	16%	15%	8%	6%	7%
1–3	20%	26%	33%	30%	19%	6%	14%
4–6	15%	19%	24%	21%	27%	35%	30%
7–9	16%	22%	13%	18%	11%	6%	9%
10–12	10%	9%	9%	9%	8%		5%
13+	26%	10%	4%	7%	27%	47%	35%

a Data were missing for 2 cases, 1 each from CC experimental unit and WVDOW control. The only significant difference in these data is for totals across the 3 sites. Chi-square = 36.99 (10 degrees of freedom) $p \leq .001$

percent of the sample at IDCFS and 56 percent at Catholic Charities but only 12 percent in West Virginia. Approximately 11 percent of the families in Illinois had Spanish surnames. There were no Asian or American Indian families in our sample. Two families from the IDCFS sample (1%) were categorized as other.

Family Size There were one or two children in more than one-half of the families (57% at IDCFS; 56% at Catholic Charities; and 63% at West Virginia), and three or four children in roughly one-third of families (33%, IDCFS; 35%, CC; and 30%, WVDOW). Ten percent of the families served in the state of Illinois and 6 percent served in West Virginia had five or more children.

Sex of Children The percentage of male and female children reported to IDCFS and Catholic Charities was fairly even, with slightly more males in the sample (51% at IDCFS and 54% at Catholic Charities). In West Virginia, 36 percent of the children were males and 64 percent were females.

Family Employment We were not able to obtain data regarding parental education nor could we obtain data on family income for most cases. Of those families on whom we have employment information, 71 percent served by IDCFS were not employed, as were 67 percent served by Catholic Charities, and 70 percent from the WVDOW.

Training Workers for the Field Test

Training of line workers and supervisors began in December 1980. Each experimental unit was trained separately following one two-hour group meeting during which all workers were oriented to the project and given copies of the training materials.[24] The duration of training sessions varied according to unit size with approximately one and one-half hours of training for every five workers in a unit. The purpose of the training sessions is described here.

Session 1

We elicited feedback from staff on decision-making materials and endeavored to clarify any misunderstandings. Procedures for using the material were described in relation to a hypothetical case.

Sessions 2 and 3

Prior to these meetings, two workers in each unit independently applied the decision-making materials to one of their active cases. During training sessions workers described their efforts to apply the experimental procedures. Strengths and weaknesses of the material were highlighted, allowing for revisions.

Session 4

Prior to this session, two workers in each unit independently pilot-tested the materials on one of their new cases. As in sessions 2 and 3, workers described their efforts to use the decision-making procedures, allowing for final revisions before the field test.

Consultation with Project Workers and Supervisors

Research staff held group consultations with project workers and supervisors once each month subsequent to implementation of the field test. The purpose of these meetings was to review worker efforts to use the decision-making materials and to resolve any difficulties that staff were having in using the procedures.

Resolution of problems could occur in one of two ways. The first took the form of additional training which focused on the workers' understanding of the project materials and on their application of these materials to cases. An additional method of resolving problems was to modify our procedures based on staff identification of weaknesses.

Reliability

Reliability tests were conducted at three points in time. Time one (T1) followed development of the decision-making material but preceded implementation of the field test. Time two (T2) and Time three (T3) occurred at the end of four and eight months of field testing.

Training of Judges

The judges were two MSW graduate students, one of whom had two years of experience in child welfare; the other, one year.[25] Training offered prior to the first reliability test proceeded as follows: each student-judge was given a copy of the decision-making material that was later used to train agency workers for the field test. They were asked to read the material prior to the first of three training-practice sessions which lasted a total of 12 hours over a three-week period of time.

Each training session began with a question-and-answer period. Next, using vignettes created for training purposes, judges worked independently applying the decision-making criteria to case material. For each decision made, student-judges were asked to state the rationale for their choice. This material was used as the basis for discussions following each session. Discussions focused on decisions that involved disagreement.

Reliability Testing

A total of 40 vignettes were created for the reliability tests. Each vignette represented a case for which nine decisions had to be made.[26] The vignettes were structured so that the information base for making each decision varied in relation to the information likely to be available to a worker at the time the decision is made in practice.[27] For example, the decision is an immediate response necessary to a report of abuse or neglect? is made on the basis of minimal information that a hot line worker has received from a reporter. By contrast, decisions such as Is there credible evidence of abuse or neglect? and

What are the problems for which the family will receive services? require more detailed data. Case information was presented on forms that had been developed for use during the field test.

Student-judges worked independently. At T1 they used the decision-making materials they had been given for training. This material was available for reference purposes during the testing periods. There was a total of 16 hours of testing spread over eight days.

T2 and T3:   Revised decision-making material was given out one week prior to the testing periods. Modifications that had been made were highlighted. Student-judges were asked to review all material with particular attention to modifications.

For eight of the nine decisions (see table 5-9) judges were asked to respond with a yes or no answer. The exception was the decision What are the specific problems for which the family will receive services? Here, problems were to be identified and ranked for each case. The extent of agreement/disagreement was determined by comparing problems identified and rankings assigned.

Results

Results are shown in table 5-8. The level of agreement at each time period was significantly greater than chance.

A somewhat different picture emerges when the extent of agreement for each time period is reviewed separately for each decision (table 5-9). Inter-judge agreement was high for six of the nine decisions, but relatively low for the decisions Is the child in immediate danger?, Is there credible evidence of abuse or neglect?, and Is the family eligible for voluntary services? Agreement/disagreement with the decision Can the child be safeguarded at home? must be viewed in relation to the decision Is the child in immediate danger? When judges agreed on the latter decision, they tended to agree on the decision regarding safety at home.

To understand why reliability was relatively low for three of the decisions it is useful to consider the process that was followed in selecting options. The decision-making criteria fall into one of two categories. In the first of these categories, criterion items were formulated in a checklist. For example, the checklist that was used to determine whether to petition the court asked Is there credible evidence of abuse or neglect? If yes, Is the parent willing to cooperate with protective services? If there was an affirmative answer to question number one, and a negative response to question number two, instructions directed the decision maker to file a court petition. Instructions were similar

TABLE 5-8. Number of Decisions on Which Judges Agreed and Disagreed for Three Time Periods

		Time One		
		Judge 1		
		Yes	No	Total
	Yes	37	14	51
Judge 2	No	18	21	39
	Total*	55	35	90

		Time Two		
		Judge 1		
		Yes	No	Total
	Yes	46	9	55
Judge 2	No	17	18	35
	Total**	63	27	90

		Time Three		
		Judge 1		
		Yes	No	Total
	Yes	40	16	56
Judge 2	No	13	21	34
	Total***	53	37	90

*Chi-Square (Corrected for Continuity) $= 5.42 \; p \leq .05$
**Chi-Square (Corrected for Continuity) $= 10.90 \; p \leq .001$
***Chi-Square (Corrected for Continuity) $= 8.31 \; p \leq .01$

if the information contained in the vignette showed that protective services had been offered in the past on a voluntary basis and that the parent withdrew from services.

When criteria are formatted in this manner, the decision maker can determine with relative ease whether any one or more of the conditions exists by cross-referencing items from the criteria checklist with the information provided in the vignette.

In contrast, to decide whether a child is in immediate danger, judges had first to determine whether any one of three general conditions was present. (The conditions dealt with supervision, the child's physical and emotional state, and the child's home.) For any condition identified, whether a series of additional factors were present had to be determined. Here, decision rules take

TABLE 5-9. Agreement and Disagreement for Each Decision for Three Time Periods for 10 Vignettes in Each Time Period

| | Times | | | | | |
| | One | | Two | | Three | |
	Agree	Disagree	Agree	Disagree	Agree	Disagree
1. Immediate home visit	9	1	9	1	8	2
2. Assistance Needed	10	0	9	1	10	0
3. Immediate danger	3	7	6	4	5	5
4. Safeguard at home	3	7	5	5	5	5
5. Credible evidence*	5	5	6	4	5	5
6. Eligible voluntary services	5	5	5	5	4	6
7. Specific problems	6	4	6	4	7	3
8. Out-of-home placement	9	1	8	2	8	2
9. Petition court	8	2	10	0	9	1
Totals	58	32	64	26	61	29

*None of the vignettes described cases where evidence was clear-cut such as when a physician has determined that an injury could not have been sustained by accident.

the form of: If yes to 1 and 2, if maybe to 3, and if no to 4. . . . In short, the worker must manipulate a great deal of information relative to other decisions and in relation to complex rules.

Retesting of Three Decisions

The following was done to deal with the low reliability attained for the three decisions. First, two checklists were developed. Each one highlighted the key issues to be considered in deciding whether a child was in immediate danger or whether there was credible evidence of maltreatment. Use of these checklists did not lead directly to decisions as was the case with the other checklists. Rather, each item served to cue the student-judges to seek information in areas relevant to each decision. This information was to be abstracted from the vignette, narrowing the universe of data to be manipulated. Next, three additional one-hour training sessions were provided. The focus was on the development and use of risk hypotheses[28] which were essential to deciding whether a family was eligible for voluntary child welfare services.[29] Additional reliability tests were conducted.

For the decision Is the child in immediate danger?, separate vignettes for issues related to supervision, conditions of the child, and of the child's home were created. In all, ten vignettes were developed and used for each of the three sections of this decision. There were three additional testing periods. Judges were told which decision was being tested. This was followed by three additional reliability tests using ten vignettes in which the three areas were combined. Thus, in this last test, we approximated the original reliability testing conditions.

For the decisions Is there credible evidence of abuse or neglect? and Is the family eligible for child welfare services?, further testing was conducted in the same manner. The results of these tests appear in tables 5-10, 5-11, and 5-12.

Table 5-10 shows the results of the separate tests of the three conditions that might constitute danger for a child as well as the results of the final test in which vignettes combined all three conditions. The outcome of additional tests for the two remaining decisions appear in table 5-11. Table 5-12 shows student-judge agreement/disagreement for the last of the three additional reliability tests for all three decisions. The level of agreement is considerably better than chance.

Notes and References

1. As noted in chapter 4, our concern was with clinical decisions, those that often require some measure of worker judgment in selecting a final option. Decisions involving client eligibility for

TABLE 5-10.   Is the Child in Immediate Danger: Supervision Only, Conditions of the Child Only, Conditions of the Home Only, and Three Conditions Combined

	One Agree	One Disagree	Retest Two Agree	Two Disagree	Three Agree	Three Disagree
Supervision Only	6	4	8	2	8	2
Condition of the Child Only	4	6	6	4	8	2
Condition of the Home Only	8	2	10	0	10	0
Conditions Combined	6	4	6	4	8	2

TABLE 5-11.   Is There Credible Evidence of Abuse or Neglect? Is the Family Eligible for Child Welfare Services?

	One Agree	One Disagree	Retest Two Agree	Two Disagree	Three Agree	Three Disagree
Credible Evidence	6	4	6	4	6	4
Family Eligible	8	2	6	4	8	2

TABLE 5-12.   Last of Three Retests: Is Child in Immediate Danger? Is There Credible Evidence of Abuse or Neglect? Is the Family Eligible for Child Welfare Services?

		Judge 1 Yes	No	Total
	Yes	13	3	16
Judge 2	No	5	9	14
	Total	18	12	30

Chi-Square $= p \leq .02$

cash and in-kind services, where a predefined set of criteria are applied to a known set of client characteristics, were not considered.

2. Project staff worked with line workers and agency administrators to identify decisions made at intake. The final roster of decisions compared favorably with those identified by Peat, Marwick, and Mitchell from their investigation of child welfare practice (see *System of Social Services for Children and Their Families: Detailed Design* (Washington, D.C.: U.S. Dept. of Health, Education and Welfare, DHEW Publication No. (OHDS) 78-30131, 1978) and with those identified by the New England Resource Center for Protective Services (see, Charles Dickinson and Carolyn Friedman, "Proposed Conceptual Framework for Intake Decision-Making: A Review of the PMM/CWLA Model" (unpublished).

3. U.S. Bureau of the Census, *Current Population Reports,* Series P-25, No. 875 (Washington, D.C.: U.S. Government Printing Office, 1980).

4. The percentage is greater than 100 because some Hispanic people are double-counted as both white or black and Hispanic. "1980 Population Statistics for the City of Chicago," prepared by the Northeastern Illinois Planning Commission.

5. Mark Testa and Fred Wolczyn, *The State of the Child,* (Chicago: The Children's Policy Research Project, 1980), pp. 34–38.

6. Charles A. Rapp, *"Effect of the Availability of Family Support Services on Decisions about Child Placement,"* Social Work Research and Abstracts, Vol. 18, No. 1 (Spring 1982), p. 22.

7. Ibid.

8. Ibid.

9. The system for handling investigations was changed part way through the project when child protective service investigative teams were created. Teams, which included social work staff, an investigator, and a nurse whose task it was to assist in evaluation of medical aspects of abuse and neglect, were made responsible for all investigations except those involving reports of sexual abuse and police-initiated protective custody. The latter were to be handled by workers from the geographic teams. See *Child Abuse and Neglect Investigation Decision Handbook* (Springfield, Illinois: Illinois Dept. of Children and Family Services, July 1982). The model described here was not implemented at Catholic Charities.

10. "Credible evidence means that the available facts when viewed in light of the surrounding circumstances would cause a reasonable person to believe that a child had been abused or neglected." Ibid. p. 33.

11. Cases could be closed even if there was credible evidence if there was no reason to assume ongoing risk and the family did not want services.

12. Testa and Wolczyn, op cit., pp. 42–44.

13. "State Rural Profile Sheet and West Virginia Advance Counts: Region VII Development Program," Region VII Planning and Development Council, (mimeographed), 1979–1980, p. 7.

14. Ibid., p. 8.

15. Ibid.

16. J. C. Dillan, Jr., ed., and Bethel Adkins and Carl Lilly, assoc. eds., *West Virginia Blue Book* (Charleston, West Virginia: Jarrett Printing Co., 1980), p. 1052.

17. "Title XX Comprehensive Annual Services Program Plan for the State of West Virginia," prepared by the West Virginia Dept. of Welfare, July 1, 1980, pp. 71, 76, 83, and 98.

18. Demographic information was collected by project staff. Each time a case was assigned to a participating worker, a research assistant abstracted relevant information from the case file.

19. Because of the time commitment required by the project, we had requested that all staff be volunteers. Lack of interest by a sufficient number of staff resulted in the administrative selection process.

20. The number of cases carried by participating workers was negotiated with administrators,

supervisors, and line workers. Project cases became a part of each worker's caseload. But, intake staff at IDCFS and Catholic Charities do not carry an ongoing caseload in the usual sense of the term. Rather, cases move through these units within 48 hours and are transferred to a service worker if there is evidence to substantiate maltreatment. Service workers at Catholic Charities and at the WVDOW carried an average of 20 cases.

21. A new case was defined as one that had not received services from one of the participating agencies in the two years prior to the project.

22. The contract between the IDCFS and Catholic Charities called for the latter to handle neglect and minor abuse cases.

23. The categories of maltreatment are based on the reporting form used by the IDCFS. Categories are not mutually exclusive since some refer to process (for example, excessive corporal punishment and torture) while others refer to the outcomes of these behaviors in terms of their effects on children, e.g., bruises, cuts, wounds, etc.

24. See Theodore J. Stein and Tina L. Rzepnicki, *Decision Making at Child Welfare Intake: A Handbook for Social Workers,* Child Welfare League of America, 1983.

25. In terms of education and experience, student-judges compare favorably with workers practicing around the country. See Ann W. Shyne and Anita G. Schroeder, *National Study of Social Services to Children and Their Families* (Washington, D.C.: U.S. Dept. of Health, Education and Welfare, DHEW Publication No. (OHDS) 78-30150, 1978), pp. 76–81.

26. The decision What is the appropriate long-range case goal? was not subject to reliability testing. This, because of directives in agency policy stating, for example, that when protective services is initiated the goal must be to maintain the child at home. If emergency placement is required, family reunification must be the goal. Thus, the goal is determined by the decision as to where the child will be living.

27. The vignettes were structured to look like case records. Information was recorded on forms like those workers would use to describe the contents of a child abuse report or those they would use to record information regarding a client's service history.

28. The worker's task is threefold. Problem specification, identification of the likely effects to a child(ren), and identification of ways to mitigate problems. For example, assume that there is evidence that a parent uses barbiturates and amphetamines. Frequency is not known. The parent's work attendance is good. When under the influence, however, he does not supervise his 6-year-old nor is the child fed on a regular basis. It is reasonable to assume that the youngster is at risk of physical injury or ill health. There are neither relatives nor neighbors to assist. Services whereby a regular child care plan can be established are called for.

29. See Stein and Rzepnicki, op cit.

6 THE PROCESS OF DECISION MAKING

For each decision made by workers in experimental and control units, the workers completed a form reporting information descriptive of the decision-making process. Whether decisions were made by the worker or another, whether clients participated in decision making, the amount of time spent reaching decisions, and the time spent on a series of decision-making activities such as gathering data are examples of what was reported. This information is presented in this chapter.

Decisions Made by Workers and by Others: An Overview

Nine clinical decisions could have been made for each case. These are (1) Is an emergency response necessary?[1] (2) Is the child in immediate danger? (3) Can the child be safeguarded at home or is protective custody necessary? (4) Is there credible evidence of abuse or neglect? (5) Is assistance required with the investigation or assessment process? (6) Is it necessary to petition the court? (7) Will the child be left at home or placed in foster care? (8) What are the specific problems for which services are necessary? and (9) What is the

99

most appropriate case plan? The decision Is an emergency response necessary? is omitted from this analysis for Illinois because this determination was made by hotline workers at the state's central registry. It is subject to supervisory review but it is not a worker decision. This was not the case in West Virginia where a reception worker determines whether an emergency response is necessary before transferring a case for an investigation.

The number and percentage of each decision that was (1) made by others, (2) not made because a case was closed, (3) never considered, and (4) made by project workers is shown in tables 6-1 (Catholic Charities), 6-2 (IDCFS), and 6-3 (WVDOW). Also reported is the number and percentage of cases where workers in experimental units used the decision-making procedures. The total number of cases that will concern us in this analysis appears in the far right-hand column of each table.

In reviewing these data, there are several points to bear in mind. At both the IDCFS and Catholic Charities the functions we define as intake were divided between two units. Intake workers at the public agency are responsible for deciding whether a child is in immediate danger, whether a child can be safeguarded at home, and whether there is credible evidence of abuse or neglect. Workers may choose to ask for assistance with the investigative process and they may consider whether it is necessary to petition the court. Decisions to place a child in out-of-home care (other than on an emergency, protective custody basis), those resulting in a determination of specific problems for which services will be provided, and case-planning decisions are in the province of the geographic teams (see ch. 5, pages 118 through 122 for a discussion of the unit functions at each test site). As noted in chapter 5, we do not have information describing the decision-making process for team workers.

The situation at Catholic Charities was similar. However, staff in that agency collaborated with their colleagues before transferring a case. The data in table 6-1 are for Catholic Charities intake workers only. Information on decisions made by service workers is reported at a later point in this chapter.

In almost all cases, some percentage of the decisions are made by others, some are not made because a case is closed, while others are not considered. Of the total decisions made (columns 1 and 4: tables 6-1 through 6-3), workers to whom a case is assigned are the primary decision makers, bearing responsibility for between 82 percent of decisions made at the IDCFS (table 6-2) to 97 percent of the decisions made at West Virginia control (table 6-3). Workers used the experimental decision-making procedures for a majority of the decisions they made (range, 71%, IDCFS to 100%, C C and W V).[2] There were no significant differences in types of decisions made by experimental and control workers at West Virginia or Catholic Charities (column 4) nor any

TABLE 6-1. Decisions Made by Others, Not Made, Not Considered Plus Decisions for Which Experimental Procedures Were Not Used and Total Number and Percentage of Decisions that Form the Basis for Data Analysis: Catholic Charities[a]

Decisions[b]	Made by Other		Not Made Case Closed		Not Considered		Made by Worker		Exp. Proc. Not Used	Total No. of Decisions	
	Exp.	Cont.	Exp.	Cont.	Exp.	Cont.	Exp.	Cont.		Exp.	Cont.
ID	15 (25%)	22 (39%)					44 (75%)	35 (61%)	3 (7%)	41 (93%)	35 (100%)
H/PC	6 (10%)	19 (33%)					53 (90%)	38 (67%)	4 (8%)	49 (92%)	38 (100%)
AR	1 (2%)	5 (9%)			54 (92%)	45 (79%)	4 (6%)	7 (12%)		4 (100%)	7 (100%)
PC	2 (3%)				29 (49%)	18 (32%)	28 (47%)	39 (68%)	3 (11%)	25 (89%)	39 (100%)
CE	5 (8%)	10 (18%)					54 (92%)	47 (82%)	6 (11%)	48 (89%)	47 (100%)
H/FC	1 (2%)	1 (2%)					58 (98%)	56 (98%)	3 (5%)	55 (95%)	56 (100%)
PR.[c]	3 (7%)		22 (51%)	22 (61%)			18 (42%)	14 (39%)	3 (17%)	15 (83%)	14 (100%)
SP	15 (28%)	7 (16%)	22 (41%)	22 (51%)			17 (31%)	14 (33%)	2 (12%)	15 (88%)	14 (100%)

[a] 59 cases were assigned to experimental units: 57 to control. The number of cases and the number of decisions are equal.

[b] ID=Child in immediate danger; H/PC=Child at home versus protective custody; AR=Assistance needed with the investigation or assessment; PC=Petition the court; CE=Credible evidence of abuse or neglect; H/FC=Child left at home or placed in foster care; PR=Specific problems for which the family requires assistance; SP=Appropriate service plan.

[c] Made collaboratively with service workers. The number is less than for other decisions because there were some cases where these decisions had not been made when the project ended. All percentages are to horizontal totals. The total number of decisions (Far right-hand column is shown as a percentage of all decisions made by worker [Column 4].) The difference between experimental and control for decisions by worker; n.s.

TABLE 6-2. Decisions Made by Others, Not Made, Not Considered Plus Decisions for Which Experimental Procedures Were Not Used and Total Number and Percentage of Decisions That Form the Basis for Data Analysis: Illinois Department of Children and Family Services[a]

Decision[b]	Made by Other	Decision Not Made Case Closed	Decision Not Considered	Made by Worker	Exp. Proc. Not Used	Total No. of Decisions
ID	9 (19%)		2 (4%)	39 (81%)	5 (13%)	34 (87%)
H/PC	12 (25%)			34 (71%)	7 (21%)	27 (79%)
AR	6 (13%)		28 (58%)	14 (29%)	4 (29%)	10 (71%)
PC	1 (2%)		47 (98%)			
CE	1 (2%)			47 (98%)	3 (6%)	44 (94%)
H/FC		18 (38%)	30 (63%)c	0		

[a] 48 cases were assigned to two experimental intake units. The number of cases and the number of decisions are equal.

[b] ID=Child in immediate danger; H/PC=Child at home versus protective custody; A.R.=Assistance needed with the investigation or assessment; PC=Petition the court; CE=Credible evidence of abuse or neglect; H/FC=Child at home or in foster care. Decisions regarding out-of-home placement, specific problems for which the family will receive assistance and case planning decisions are not made by workers in intake units. All percentages are to horizontal totals. Total number of decisions [Far right-hand column] is shown as a percentage of all decisions made by the worker [Column 4].

c This decision would be made by the worker in the geographic team to whom the case was transferred.

TABLE 6-3. Decisions Made by Others, Not Made, Not Considered Plus Decisions for Which Experimental Procedures Were Not Used and Total Number and Percentage of Decisions That Form the Basis for Data Analysis: West Virginia Department of Welfare[a]

	Decision										
	Made by Other		Not Made Case Closed		Not Considered		Made by Worker		Exp. Proc. Not Used	Total No. of Decisions	
Decision[b]	Exp.	Cont.	Exp.	Cont.	Exp.	Cont.	Exp.	Cont.		Exp.	Cont.
ER[c]	1 (4%)	2 (13%)					23 (96%)	13 (87%)		23 (100%)	13 (100%)
ID	3 (16%)	1 (7%)					16 (84%)	14 (93%)	2 (13%)	14 (87%)	14 (100%)
H/PC	1 (4%)				1 (4%)		18 (96%)	15 (100%)	3 (17%)	15 (83%)	15 (100%)
AR	1 (4%)				14 (74%)	11 (73%)	4 (21%)	4 (27%)	1 (25%)	3 (75%)	4 (100%)
PC					6 (32%)		13 (68%)	15 (100%)	3 (23%)	10 (77%)	15 (100%)
CE	1 (4%)						18 (96%)	15 (100%)	4 (22%)	14 (78%)	15 (100%)
H/FC			10 (53%)	11 (73%)			9 (47%)	4 (27%)	1 (11%)	8 (89%)	4 (100%)
PR	1 (4%)		16 (84%)	12 (80%)			2 (11%)	3 (20%)		2 (100%)	3 (100%)
SP			16 (84%)	12 (80%)			3 (16%)	3 (20%)		2 (100%)	3 (100%)

[a] Nineteen cases were assigned to experimental; 15 to control. The number of cases and the number of decisions are equal.

[b] ER = Emergency response; ID = Child in immediate danger; H/PC = Child at home versus protective custody; CE = Credible evidence of abuse or neglect; AR = Assistance needed with the assessment or investigation; PC = Petition the court; H/FC = Child at home or in foster care; PR = Specific problems for which the family will receive assistance; SP = Appropriate service plan.

[c] n for this decision is Exp. = 11; Cont. = 5. This is due to the fact that some reports were received by a reception worker who did not participate in the project. Assignment of cases as experimental or control was made after cases came to the reception worker.

Percentages are to horizontal totals. Total number of decisions [Far right-hand column] is shown as a percentage of all decisions made by worker [Column 4]. Differences between experimental and control groups for decisions made by worker; n.s.

significant differences between experimental units across test sites for the three decisions common to these sites (immediate danger, home/protective custody, and credible evidence).

Whether a case is opened to protective services is contingent upon whether there is credible evidence of maltreatment. If evidence exists problem assessment and case planning take place.[3] If a case is not opened to protective service, but a family wants assistance, their case may be transferred to the agency's voluntary service program. At Catholic Charities (table 6-1), 22 of the 59 cases referred to the experimental unit (37%) and an equal number of the 57 referred to control (39%) were closed subsequent to the investigation. The majority of cases are closed at West Virginia (table 6-3). Eighty-four percent of those in the experimental unit (16 of 19) and 80 percent of those in control (12 of 15) were closed. Closing a majority of cases is normative practice in West Virginia.[4] At IDCFS there was a determination of credible evidence for 20 cases, 18 were closed, and the remainder were sent to a geographic team for completion of the investigation.

Decisions Not Considered

Whether to ask for assistance with the investigation and whether to petition the court were not considered in a near majority of cases across sites. Workers reported that they do not consider petitioning the court unless parents are not cooperating. Cooperation was reported for 75 percent to 100 percent of all cases.

Requests for medical examinations of children account for 85 percent of all assistance required across sites and units. Psychological examinations (at Catholic Charities and West Virginia) and police assistance in gaining access to a home at the IDCFS account for the remaining requests.

It is of interest to note the similarities and differences across sites in decisions routinely made during intake. Regardless of the site, a determination of the need for an emergency response is made separately from other decisions by the person responsible for receiving the report. In Illinois, responsibility for this decision falls on a hotline worker located in the state capital in Springfield. In West Virginia, a reception worker within the agency makes this decision.

This decision is reviewed when the report is received at the regional office in Chicago. We do not have data on time spent in such review nor do we know how frequently the decision is reversed. There is a duplication of effort. Whether this is an efficient use of time is an empirical question that can only be answered with data showing the frequency with which decisions are changed and risk to children reduced as a consequence of change.

West Virginia workers did not report routine review of this decision. The fact that both reception and investigative workers at this site are housed in the same facility and have easy access to each other could result in an informal exchange of information as a substitute for a more distinctive review process. Or, workers may trust the judgment of their colleagues whom they know and may therefore be less likely to engage in a review process.

Across sites and units, three decisions are always considered: Is the child in immediate danger?, Is protective custody necessary?, and Is there credible evidence of abuse or neglect? Whether assistance is needed wtih investigatory tasks and whether to petition the court are considered only if some characteristic of the case, (an observable injury on a child, for example, or lack of cooperation by parents), cue the worker to the need for diagnostic aid or court assistance.

Five of the nine decisions that could be made at intake bear directly on an agency's mandate to investigate reports of maltreatment. Decisions regarding an emergency response, immediate danger, whether protective custody is necessary, whether assistance is needed or a court petition must be filed, may be viewed as links in a chain, each contributing information to the determination of whether there is credible evidence of abuse or neglect. This latter decision marks the end point of the investigative process. Subsequent decisions, beginning with a determination of whether foster home care is necessary, may be viewed in the context of an agency's service function. Differences across sites in decisions considered by intake staff are most apparent at the end point in the investigative process.

IDCFS intake staff, whose role is conceptualized by administration as investigatory,[5] never reported having considered the decision Will the child remain at home or be placed in foster care? This option would be addressed by workers in geographic teams whose main function is service provision. Catholic Charities represents the opposite end of the spectrum. The worker's role is seen in terms of both investigatory and service-delivery tasks. Intake workers do not provide services over time. However, the worker's orientation to her role includes both an investigatory and a service set. Catholic Charities intake staff collaborated with their colleagues in service units on decisions regarding home versus foster care placement before closing a case for 98 percent of all cases.

In West Virginia, worker decision making is influenced mostly by an investigative model. Half of the cases in experimental units and nearly three-quarters of those in control were closed following a determination of credible evidence. The decision regarding foster home care was considered by intake staff only for those cases where there was evidence of maltreatment. We will return to the subject of role orientation in the next section where data on time spent in decision-making activities are reported and in chapter 8 where the implications of the project are addressed.

Within test sites, the average number of decisions made by experimental and control staff is approximately the same (table 6-4). IDCFS workers averaged fewer decisions per case (2.8) than did staff at Catholic Charities (4.7 experimental; 4.4. control) and West Virginia (5.6 experimental; 5.9 control).

Decisions Made by Others

The first question that we asked workers was whether they or someone else made each decision. If made by another, staff were asked to report who the decision maker was, whether or not they agreed with the option selected, and, in the event of disagreement, why this was so.

As a percentage of all decisions, those made by others accounts for between 15 percent and 20 percent at Catholic Charities experimental and control, respectively, and 18 percent for IDCFS. The percentages are much smaller in West Virginia where 6 percent of experimental decisions and 3 percent of those in control are made by others. The differences btween experimental and control units at Catholic Charities and West Virginia are not significant. However,

TABLE 6-4. Average Number of Decisions per Case Made by Experimental and Control Intake Workers and Average Number Made Using Experimental Decision-Making Procedures: Three Test Sites

Site	Maximum Number of Decisions Made at Site[a]	Average Made by Workers	
		Overall[b]	Using Exp. Procedures
IDCFS	5	2.8	2.4
(n = 48)			
Catholic Charities			
EXP. (n = 59)	8	4.7	4.3
CONT. (n = 57)	8	4.4	
West Virginia			
EXP. (n = 19)	9	5.6	4.9
CONT. (n = 15)	9	5.7	

[a] See Tables 6-1, 6-2, and 6-3 for a listing of decisions.
[b] See Column 4, Tables 6-1, 6-2, and 6-3.
[c] See Column 6, Tables 6-1, 6-2, and 6-3.

there are significant differences between experimental units across the three test sites (Chi-square $= 7.843$, 2 degrees of freedom, $p \leq .02$).

Other decision makers are either workers and supervisors within one's own agency or persons external to the agency (table 6-5). Persons in the latter category account for the majority of other decision makers in Illinois (range $= 65\%$, Catholic Charities control to 81%, IDCFS) but only 40 percent and 42 percent of others in West Virginia, experimental and control, respectively. Decisions made by persons outside of the agency are generally made before the worker receives a case. They are most likely to be those decisions made early in the investigation such as Is the child in immediate danger? and Is protective custody necessary? In the WV sample, the actual number of decisions made by others is quite low. The greatest percentage in any one category involve immediate danger, accounting for 43 percent of those in experimental and 33 percent in control (table 6-6). Taken together, decisions regarding immediate danger and protective custody account for between 44 percent of decisions in Catholic Charities experimental to 72 percent of decisions made at the IDCFS.

TABLE 6-5. Number and Percentage of Other Decision Makers for Protective Service Cases at Three Test Sites

			Site		
	IDCFS	CC			WVDOW
	Exp.	Exp.	Cont	Exp.	Cont.
Decision Maker[a]	(n=21)	(n=38)	(n=48)	(n=7)	(n=5)
Police	3 (14%)	9 (24%)	8 (17%)		2 (40%)
Juvenile Court Judge		1 (3%)			
Hospital[b]	9 (43%)	7 (18%)	9 (19%)	1 (14%)	
Other Social Service Agency[c]	1 (5%)	5 (13%)	4 (8%)	1 (14%)	
Supervisor	3 (14%)	5 (13%)	13 (27%)		2 (40%)
Co-Worker	1 (5%)	3 (8%)	4 (8%)	4 (57%)	1 (20%)
Other[d]	4 (19%)	8 (21%)	10 (21%)	1 (14%)	

[a] Data were missing on 4 IDCFS intake decisions and on 2 from the control unit at Catholic Charities.

[b] Includes doctor, nurse, and hospital social worker.

[c] Includes public aide workers and IDCFS workers.

[d] Includes court personnel such as probation officers and state attorney, school personnel, family members, and unspecified others. Chi-Square for Catholic Charities (police, hospital, supervisor, and other decision makers)$=2.394$ (3 degrees of freedom) n.s. Other cell frequencies are too small for tests of significance.

TABLE 6-6. Number and Percentage of Decisions Made by Another by Type of Decision for Protective Service Cases Across Three Test Sites

Decision	IDCFS Exp. (n=29)	CC Exp. (n=48)	CC Cont. (n=64)	W. Va. Exp. (n=7)	W. Va. Cont. (n=3)
Emergency Response				1 (14%)	2 (67%)
Immediate Danger	9 (31%)	15 (31%)	22 (34%)	3 (43%)	1 (33%)
Home or Prot. Cust.	12 (41%)	6 (13%)	19 (30%)		
Credible Evidence	1 (3%)	5 (10%)	10 (16%)	1 (14%)	
Assist. Required	6 (21%)	1 (2%)	5 (8%)	1 (14%)	
Petition Court	1 (3%)	2 (4%)			
Home/Fost. Care		1 (2%)	1 (2%)		
Specific Problems		3 (6%)		1 (14%)	
Service Plans		15 (31%)	7 (11%)		

That these decisions are the ones most often made by others and that other decision makers are most likely to be hospital staff or police personnel (table 6-5) is not surprising. Some percentage of protective service reports are made directly to the police department and, in the context of responding to reports of domestic violence, police may identify children at risk. Medical personnel, especially those in hospital emergency rooms, identify some percentage of all cases of maltreatment.

Whether there was credible evidence of maltreatment was decided by another, usually a supervisor, in 16 percent of the control cases at Catholic Charities and 10 percent of those in experimental units. Thirty-one percent of the service-planning decisions in Catholic Charities experimental unit cases were decided by another in contrast to 11 percent of those for control cases. The other was the worker to whom a case was transferred. Finally, in IDCFS cases, 21 percent of decisions made by others involved a determination that assistance was required with the investigation. Hospital staff and, to a lesser extent, supervisors were the other decision makers.

Forty-three percent of the outside decision makers involved in public agency cases in Illinois were hospital staff (table 6-5) followed by miscellaneous others (19%) and police (14%). Law enforcement personnel account for 24 percent of other decision makers in experimental cases at Catholic Charities, for 17 percent in control, and for 40 percent in the control unit at WV but for none in the experimental unit.

Twenty-one percent of other decision makers in both the experimental and control units at Catholic Charities were court and school personnel, family members, and unidentified others. In 18 percent of experimental cases and in 19 percent of those in control, hospital staff were the other decision makers.

Supervisors played a larger role as decision makers in control cases at both CC (27%) and the WVDOW (40%) than they did in experimental cases where they accounted for 13 percent at CC but made no decisions in WV. Co-workers were more active as decision makers in WV experimental unit cases, accounting for 57 percent of others compared to control where they accounted for 20 percent. At CC, 8 percent of the other decision makers in both experimental and control cases were co-workers and at IDCFS they were 5 percent of others.

Rarely did any worker disagree with decisions made by others regardless of the decision or the person who made it. It is not surprising, therefore, that workers rarely asked for clarification of the basis for reaching a decision. At Catholic Charities, however, there was a difference between groups where experimental staff asked for clarification for 29 percent of the decisions made in contrast to 8 percent for control.

Summary of Decisions Made by Workers

Four decisions are routinely made at protective service intake. Is an emergency response necessary?, Is a child in immediate danger?, Is protective custody necessary? and Is there credible evidence of maltreatment? Workers consider whether to ask for assistance with the investigation and whether to petition the court only when case-specific information such as the condition of the child or lack of parental cooperation dictate.

Whether workers make the remaining decisions is seen as a function of the investigative or service orientation of the agency regarding the responsibilities of intake staff. IDCFS most clearly represent an investigative model, CC, a service model, and the WVDOW, a mixed orientation.

Others are involved in making some case decisions. However, the worker to whom a case is assigned is the primary decision maker. When decisions are made by persons external to the agency, they are most apt to involve questions of immediate danger to children and whether protective custody is necessary.

It is not surprising that hospital and police personnel make most of these decisions.

At Catholic Charities, 22 percent of the 59 cases assigned to experimental units (37%) with an equal number of the 57 assigned to control (39%) were closed at the end of the investigation. At the IDCFS, 18 cases (38%) were closed by intake workers. The remaining 30 cases were transferred to geographic teams for completion of the investigation. The greatest percentage of cases were closed in WV—80 percent of those assigned to control units, 84 percent of those assigned to experimental.

The Decision-Making Process

When workers claimed responsibility for making decisions we asked that they report (1) the frequency of contacts with collaterals and clients by method of contact for each decision; (2) whether parents and children were involved in the decision-making process and whether they agreed with the decision made; (3) the amount of time spent in each of a series of decision-making activities plus total time spent analyzing data and reaching a final decision; and (4) in those instances in which a worker received written information from another professional, whether they found the information useful for decision-making purposes, and whether they had to spend time seeking clarification of the information.

Contacts with Clients   Workers reported frequency of contact by method for each decision. We had expected that the number of contacts with clients would increase as workers proceeded through the investigation to case assessment and service planning. This was not the case. Regardless of the site or the unit, the frequency of contact with clients (as well as with collaterals) rarely increased beyond those that were made for the first decision—Is the child in immediate danger? It would appear that all decisions were made based on data gathered in the first one or two meetings with clients.

The average number of in-person contacts with clients was approximately the same for experimental unit workers at Catholic Charities and in the WVDOW (2.3, CC: 2.4, WVDOW) as it was for control workers who averaged 3.7 in-person contacts at Catholic Charities and 3.8 in-person contacts in West Virginia. IDCFS workers saw clients less frequently, averaging 1.7 in-person contacts per case.

Telephone contacts were rare. Experimental and control workers at Catholic Charities averaged one such contact per case. Their counterparts in WV, .5, and at IDCFS, .3.

Subsequent to a finding of credible evidence, Catholic Charities intake workers transferred cases to in-home or foster care service units whose workers carried primary responsibility for case assessment, service-planning decisions, and service provision. All staff in these units participated as experimental workers. We were interested in knowing whether their activities were affected by the case originating in an experimental or a control intake unit.

Frequency of contact with clients was much higher for service workers than for intake staff. Frequency varied, however, as a function of whether a case came from an experimental or a control intake worker. The average number of in-person contacts for cases coming from experimental workers was 4.8 compared to an average of 6.5 for cases coming from control. The average number of telephone contacts varied as well from a low of 1.9 for cases coming from an experimental worker to a high of 2.7 for those that came from control. The differences, which were not statistically significant, may be due to the quality of the data gathered by experimental workers which service staff rated more useful than the data they usually received when cases were transferred. As we will see in the next section, service workers spent significantly less time clarifying data coming from an experimental intake worker than they did in this activity when data came from control.

Parents Participated in making decisions on 50 percent to 75 percent of all cases. Involvement by children occurred on a smaller scale, not exceeding 20 percent of all cases. Regardless of the site, the unit, or the decision made, parental cooperation was reported as the norm. Parents were said to be very willing or willing to cooperate on between 75 percent and 100 percent of all cases.

Contacts with Collaterals Catholic Charities and WVDOW workers had contacts with collaterals in the majority of cases, ranging from 63 percent of those at Catholic Charities (experimental and control) to between 53 percent and 93 percent of cases in West Virginia, experimental and control, respectively. At IDCFS contacts with collaterals occurred for 29 percent of cases. The fact that our data were reported by workers from the evening and midnight shifts (4 P.M. to 6 A.M., inclusively) whose access to teachers and social workers in other agencies was limited, may explain this finding.

The average number of contacts was similar across sites and units, ranging from a low of 2 contacts for West Virginia control to a high of 2.6 for Catholic Charities control.

Contacts were almost equally divided between in-person and telephone for all groups except the experimental intake unit at Catholic Charities who reported a smaller percentage of in-person contacts (34%) than telephone contacts which accounted for 65 percent of those made.

Service workers at Catholic Charities contacted collaterals on 43 percent of the cases coming from experimental and on 60 percent of those coming from control intake workers. Staff averaged three contacts per case for those originating in experimental units of which 21 percent were made in-person and 79 percent by phone, and five contacts per case on those from control of which 45 percent were in-person and 32 percent by phone.

Medical personnel were contacted more frequently than any other group of collaterals by all workers except for those serving experimental unit cases in West Virginia. For workers in the latter unit, contacts with medical staff ranked second to those made with school personnel, which accounted for 57 percent of contacts made. Educators ranked second as a source of information for control staff in West Virginia, third for cases at Catholic Charities, and fourth for those in the IDCFS.

Social workers in other agencies were contacted frequently by staff at Catholic Charities and at the IDCFS but played a relatively minor role in West Virginia cases. IDCFS workers and those in the control group at West Virginia contacted police frequently although experimental unit staff in West Virginia did not. Finally, neighbors were seen with some frequency by workers in West Virginia and at the IDCFS.

Service workers at Catholic Charities made most of their collateral contacts with social workers at other agencies. Medical personnel ranked second for cases coming from control workers. Contacts with school staff and miscellaneous others, accounting for 25 percent and 29 percent of contacts made, are nearly tied for second place for experimental unit cases.

Time Spent in Decision Making

For each decision made, workers reported the amount of time spent in each of four decision-making activities plus the time spent analyzing data and selecting a final option.

In reviewing these data the reader should be cognizant of some initial difficulties that workers had in providing exact time estimates for all activities. There are situations, for example, when a worker consults with his or her supervisor about a specific decision or when he or she meets with a family for the express purpose of observing parent–child interaction, which lend themselves to providing an accurate estimate of time in relation to a given activity. In other circumstances it is difficult to be precise. A worker who is explaining the function of protective services to a parent may also be engaging in data-gathering activities by making observations of the home situation. Several decisions may be reviewed during a supervisory consultation or discussed informally with colleagues over lunch. When this occurs, dividing time into a series of discrete categories is not easy. Over time, workers reported an increased awareness of their use of time in relation to discrete decision-making activities.

The average amount of time per case spent in each of four decision-making activities is reported in table 6-7. Time spent analyzing data and reaching a final decision appears in table 6-8. Neither table includes data for Catholic Charities service workers for whom information is reported later. At Catholic Charities and the WVDOW, staff in experimental units spent significantly less time than control workers gathering data (Catholic Charities; $p \leq .01$: West Virginia; $P \leq .05$). There were no significant differences between experimental and control workers at either site for the remaining decision-making activities.

Experimental and control staff at all sites devoted the greatest percentage of their time to acquiring information for decision making. Workers at the IDCFS, however, spent a much smaller percentage of their time in this activity than did experimental staff at other sites (29% for IDCFS compared to 40% for WV and 44% for Catholic Charities). The percentage of time that IDCFS workers spent in the various activities is more evenly divided across activities than is the case at other test sites.

Across units, time spent in formal consultation ranks next for Catholic Charities and West Virginia staff. At the IDCFS, informal consultation occupied slightly more staff time (36 minutes:27%) than did formal consultation (32 minutes: 24%).

It is interesting to note that public agency workers spent comparable amounts of time in each activity, an observation that we shall see repeated throughout these data, even though the percentage of time devoted to each activity differs. In general, workers at Catholic Charities spent greater amounts of time in all decision-related activities when compared to public agency workers. The difference between experimental units at IDCFS and West Virginia compared to those at Catholic Charities in gathering data, formal and informal consultation, and private thinking time is significant ($f = 32.366$, $p \leq .001$).

Except for out-of-home placement decisions, experimental workers in West Virginia spent significantly less time analyzing data and reaching each decision than did control staff (table 6-8). At Catholic Charities there was a significant difference between units for the decisions: Is there credible evidence of abuse or neglect? and What are the specific problems for which the family will receive services? Of all decisions, Catholic Charities workers devoted the greatest percentage of their time to problem identification, WV experimental workers to out-of-home placement decisions, and WV control staff and IDCFS workers to determining whether there was credible evidence of maltreatment. For decisions regarding immediate danger and protective custody, time reported

TABLE 6-7. Average Time per Case in Hours and Minutes Spent in Decision-Making Activities for all Decisions for Three Test Sites

Activity[c]	Catholic Charities		West Virginia		IDCFS	
	Exp. (n = 55)[b]	Cont. (n = 56)	Exp. (n = 15)	Cont. (n = 15)	Exp. (n = 44)	
Gathering Data	2:01 [44%]	3:21 [53%]*	0:47 [40%]	1:18 [57%]**	0:39 [29%]	
Consultation:						
Formal	1:31 [33%]	1:42 [27%]***	0:35 [30%]	0:35 [26%]***	0:32 [24%]	
Informal	0:33 [12%]	0:42 [11%]***	0:16 [14%]	0:00	0:36 [27%]	
Private Thinking						
Time	0:29 [11%]	0:33 [9%]***	0:19 [16%]	0:24 [18%]***	0:27 [20%]	

[a] Tests of significance are for experimental versus control at Catholic Charities and West Virginia. $*p \leq .005 **p \leq .05 ***$N.S. Time was converted to minutes to calculate percentages here and in all other tables in which time is reported.

[b] Maximum number of decisions made by experimental and control workers. See tables 6-1, 6-2, and 6-3.

[c] Time spent in each activity was averaged across all decisions for which experimental workers used the experimental decision-making procedures and for all decisions made by control staff. [See far right-hand column of Tables 6-1, 6-2, and 6-3]. Time spent making the emergency response decision in West Virginia was not included since this was the only site where intake staff had responsibility for this decision.

TABLE 6-8. Average Time per Case in Hours and Minutes to Analyze Data and to Reach Final Decisions: Three Test Sites

| Decisions[a] | Catholic Charities | | West Virginia | | IDCFS |
	Exp.	Cont.	Exp.	Cont.	Exp.
Immediate Danger Home/Prot.	1:36 [15%]	1:45 [12%]*	0:33 [17%]	1:12 [15%]**	0:40 [26%]
Custody Petition	1:30 [14%]	1:20 [10%]*	0:33 [17%]	1:19 [16%]**	0:50 [33%]
Court Credible	1:29 [14%]	2:32 [17%]*	0:40 [21%]	1:35 [19%]***	0:00
Evidence Out-of-Home	1:32 [14%]	2:32 [17%]***	0:39 [20%]	2:03 [26%]****	1:03 [41%]
Placement Problem	2:02 [19%]	2:26 [16%]*	0:40 [25%]	2:00 [24%]*	0:00
Identification	2:30 [23%]	4:25 [29%]***	0:00	0:00*****	0:00

[a] The number and percentage of each decision made by workers appears in the far right-hand column of Tables 6-1, 6-2, and 6.3.
*n.s. **$p \leq .05$ ***$p \leq .01$ ****$p \leq .001$ *****Missing Data

by experimental workers in the public agencies is comparable and, again, differs from that reported by private agency staff.

The data presented thus far are summarized in table 6-9 where time spent in each decision-making activity, time spent analyzing information and making a final decison, and the average amount of time per case spent in all decision-making activities is reported. The difference between experimental and control unit staff at the public agencies and their counterparts in the voluntary sector is dramatically illustrated in these data. Experimental staff at Catholic Charities spent more than twice the amount of time in all activities than did experimental workers in the public settings. We think that the service orientation at Catholic Charities compared to the investigatory orientation at the public agencies explains this difference.

The fact that the voluntary agency conducts investigations for an exact number of cases established by contract with the public agency supports a service orientation. Knowledge of the number of investigations to be conducted within any time period allows staff to plan their time. Given a service orientation, staff can be expected to devote some percentage of all time with clients to establishing a relationship as a precursor to providing services. We think it unlikely that the workers would be successful in separating time spent in decision-making activities from that spent in establishing a working relationship. We would speculate that the time data reported by Catholic Charities staff includes time spent in the latter activity as well as time spent in decision-making activities.

Intake workers in public settings must investigate all reports. Even though the average number of investigations within any time period can be estimated, workers know that the number can fluctuate greatly. This knowledge may create pressure for workers to complete investigations in the shortest possible time. The agency's emphasis on an investigatory as opposed to a service function support staff in taking such an approach.

Our data showed that Catholic Charities intake workers collaborated with their colleagues to whom they transferred cases on three decisions: Should a child will be left in his or her own home or be placed in foster care? What are the specific problems for which the family will receive services? and, to a lesser degree, on service-planning decisions.

In addition to time spent in collaborative decision making (reported as formal consultation in tables 6-7 and 6-9), the worker to whom a case is transferred may refer back to the intake worker for clarification of information contained in the case record and she or he may determine that data, over and above what is contained in the record, must be gathered in order to make a final decision. As was the case with intake staff, a worker receiving a case may consult with her or his supervisor, have informal discussions with colleagues,

TABLE 6-9. Average Time per Case in Hours and Minutes to Complete Four Decision-Making Activities and to Analyze Data and Reach Final Decisions

Activity[a]	Catholic Charities		West Virginia		IDCFS
	Exp. (n=55)	Cont. (n=36)	Exp. (n=15)	Cont. (n=15)	Exp. (n=44)
Gathering Data	2:01 [16%]	3:21 [19%]	0:47 [15%]	1:10 [12%]	0:39 [14%]
Consultation:					
Formal	1:31 [12%]	1:42 [10%]	0:35 [11%]	0:35 [5%]	0:32 [11%]
Informal	0:33 [4%]	0:42 [4%]	0:16 [5%]	0:00	0:36 [13%]
Private Thinking	0:29 [4%]	0:33 [4%]	0:19 [6%]	0:24 [4%]	0:27 [9%]
Analyze Data and Reach Decisions[b]	0:09 [64%]	10:72 [64%]	3:13 [62%]	8:14 [78%]	2:33 [53%]
Average Time per Case: All Activities	12:43	17:30	5:10	10:31	4:47

[a] Time spent in each activity has averaged across all decisions for which experimental workers used the experimental decision-making procedures and for all decisions made by control unit staff [See far right-hand column of Tables 6-1, 6-2, and 6-3]. Time spent in emergency response decision for WV staff was not included since this is the only site at which experimental workers made this decision.

[b] Time involved in problem identification for Catholic Charities workers was not included since this was the only site that reported time data for this decision.

and spend time thinking about each decision in addition to analyzing data and selecting a final option.

The effect, if any, on the amount of time that workers spent in these activities as a function of whether the case came from an experimental or control intake worker was of concern to us. We divided the cases carried by service workers, all of whom were experimental staff, into two categories according to the source of the referral. These data are reported in table 6-10. There are significant differences in the first three time categories (clarifying, gathering data, formal consultation), but no differences in time spent in informal consultation, private thinking time, and time spent analyzing data to make a final decision. Workers whose cases came from an experimental intake worker spent significantly less time in three of five possible activities leading to a final decision than did their colleagues whose cases came from a control worker.

TABLE 6-10. Average Time per Case in Hours and Minutes Spent in Decision-Making Activities Including Data Analysis and Reaching Final Decision by Catholic Charities' Experimental Unit Service Workers as a Function of Whether a Case Came From an Intake Experimental versus an Intake Control Unit

Activity	Unit One[a] (n = 16)	Unit Two[b] (n = 16)
Clarify Data	0:50 [13%]	1:44 [16%]*
Gather Data	1:11 [19%]	2:29 [23%]**
Consultation:		
Formal[c]	0:50 [13%]	2:34 [24%]***
Informal	0:45 [12%]	1:12 [11%]****
Private Thinking Time	0:59 [16%]	0:52 [8%]****
Reach Final Decision	1:40 [27%]	1:55 [18%]****
Average Time per Case: All Activities	6:15	10:46

[a] Cases received from an intake experimental unit
[b] Cases received from an intake control unit
[c] Includes time spent collaborating with workers from whom the case was transferred.
*$p \le .05$ **$p \le .01$ ***$p \le .001$ ****n.s.

We have noted that workers in the public agencies tended to resemble each other regarding time spent in decision making, both differing from their colleagues in the voluntary agency. This is borne out by the data in table 6-11. Time spent by all experimental workers analyzing information and reaching conclusions for the three decisions common to the sites is presented. There are significant differences between the two public agencies and the private agency for the first two decisions reported in table 6-11. For the determination of credible evidence, there is a significant difference across all three sites.

It is particularly interesting to note that, despite the significant difference between experimental units in Chicago and West Virginia, there are no significant differences for control unit staff (table 6-12).

Decisions whether to petition the court and whether out-of-home placement was called for were not made by intake workers at the IDCFS. In tables 6-13 and 6-14 we present data comparing time spent by experimental workers (table 6-13) and control workers (table 6-14) at Catholic Charities and West Virginia for these decisions. The differing amounts of time spent by voluntary agency

TABLE 6-11. Comparison of Experimental Units at Three Test Sites: Average Time per Case in Hours and Minutes to Analyze Data and to Reach Three Decisions

	Catholic Charities	IDCFS	West Virginia
Immediate Danger (CC:n =41) (IDCFS:n = 34) (WV:n = 14)	1:36	0:40	0:33*
Home: Prot. Custody (CC:n =49) (IDCFS:n =27) (WV:n = 15)	1:30	0:50	0:35*
Credible Evidence (CC:n =48) (IDCFS:n =44) (WV:n = 14)	1:32	1:03	0:39**

One-Way Analysis of Variance *$p \leq .001$ **$p \leq .01$

TABLE 6-12. Comparison of Control Units at Catholic Charities and West Virginia: Average Time per Case in Hours and Minutes to Analyze Data and to Reach a Final Decision

Decision	Catholic Charities	West Virginia
Immediate Danger (CC:$n=35$) (WV:$n=14$)	1:45	1:12*
Home Protective Custody (CC:$n=38$) (WV:$n=15$)	1:28	1:19*
Credible Evidence (CC:$n=47$) (WV:$n=15$)	2:32	2:08*

*$t=$ n.s.

TABLE 6-13. Comparison of Experimental Units at Catholic Charities and West Virginia: Average Time per Case in Hours and Minutes to Analyze Data and to Reach Decisions

Petition	Catholic Charities	West Virginia
Court (CC:$n=25$) (WV:$n=10$)	1:29	0:40*
Out-of-Home Placement (CC:$n=55$) (WV:$n=8$)	2:02	0:48*

*$t=p \leq .01$

TABLE 6-14   Comparison of Control Units at
Catholic Charities and West Virginia: Average
Time per Case in Hours and Minutes to
Analyze Data and to Reach a Decision

Petition	Catholic Charities	West Virginia
Court	2:32	1:35*
(CC:$n = 39$)		
(WV:$n = 15$)		
Out-of-Home		
Placement	2:26	2:00*
(CC:$n = 56$)		
(WV:$n = 4$)		

*$t =$ n.s.

staff compared to those in the public sector is clear from the data in table 6-13 ($p \leq .005$). Again, there were no significant differences in time between control unit workers at either site.

Summary of the Decision Making Process

Gathering data, formal consultation with supervisors, informal consultation with colleagues, and private thinking time are four activities that workers engage in prior to analyzing data and making a final decision. Of these activities, data-gathering occupied the greatest percentage of worker time across sites. Experimental workers at West Virginia and Catholic Charities spent significantly less time in this activity than their colleagues who served control unit cases. There were no significant differences between experimental and control units for other activities.

A repeated finding was that experimental unit staff in the public agencies in West Virginia and Illinois spent comparable amounts of time in all decision tasks, both differing from experimental workers in the voluntary agency. Interestingly, however, there were no significant differences between control units in WV and at CC in time spent analyzing data and reaching final decisions.

Catholic Charities service workers who received cases from experimental intake staff in their own agency spent significantly less time clarifying data they received, gathering additional data, and consulting on cases than did service workers whose cases came from control intake staff.

Notes and References

1. An emergency response is one requiring immediate action. The worker does not have the 24-hour response time permitted by law.

2. Twelve of the thirty experimental workers (40%) used the procedures for all of their cases, 11 (37%) for 75 percent of their cases, and 7 workers (23%) for between one-third and two-thirds of their cases. Worker use/nonuse of the experimental procedures as a function of worker or case characteristics is the subject of a doctoral dissertation in progress. Preliminary analysis of these data does not suggest any consistent relationship between case or worker characteristics and the use or nonuse of the experimental decision-making procedures. The authors want to thank James Gleeson for sharing his findings with us.

3. Workers may find evidence of maltreatment yet not open the case. If abuse or neglect is not serious, ongoing risk unlikely, and the family unwilling to cooperate, the case can be *indicated* —a determination that there was credible evidence—and not opened.

4. This determination is based on a comparison of project cases with the universe of cases from which they were sampled.

5. For a discussion of this subject, see *Child Abuse and Neglect Investigation Decisions Handbook* (Springfield, Illinois: Illinois Department of Children and Family Services, July 1982), pp. 9–11.

7 THE OUTCOMES OF DECISION MAKING

The Outcome of Using Structured Decision-Making Procedures

The hypotheses that guided our work and questions that concerned us were reported in chapter 5. The extent to which our data support or refute these hypotheses are discussed below.

Reliability

We assumed that inter-judge reliability would improve relative to what has been reported in the literature. Our data support this hypothesis. Inter-judge agreement was statistically significant for all decisions (see chapter 5).

We recognize the limits of generalizing these findings to the world of practice. We do not know what level of reliability would be attained in practice situations nor do we have a basis for suggesting the level of reliability, beyond pure chance, that should be acceptable. These are issues for future research.

Efficiency,

defined as the amount of time spent in decision-making activities, should be greater using a structured approach to decision making than it is using an unstructured approach.[1] Moreover, workers who receive cases from staff using experimental decision-making procedures should spend less time in decision-making activities than workers whose cases come from control. Both of these hypotheses are supported by our data.

Service Planning

If the use of structured decision-making procedures was more efficient, we assumed that service plans would be formulated at an earlier point in time in experimental units than in control. The fact that agency policy came to require the formulation of service plans within 30 days of the time a case was opened precluded the likelihood that this hypothesis would bear fruit.

Recidivism[2]

Whether the recidivism rate would differ for cases served by experimental staff when compared to those served by control workers was another question asked. In Illinois, recidivism data were obtained for all cases assigned to the project by running client identification numbers through the central computer approximately six months after completion of the field test. In West Virginia cases were checked manually.

There were no recidivist cases in West Virginia. At Catholic Charities, the number of cases for which a second report was received was equal for experimental and control with four cases from each unit. At the IDCFS, there were two recidivist cases from those assigned to experimental units and four from those assigned to control units. The hypothesis that use of structured decision-making procedures affects recidivism is not supported by our data.

Decision Outcomes

Whether there would be any differences between units in the numbers of children said to be in immediate danger, placed in protective custody, differences in findings of credible evidence, and in children placed in out-of-home care was another area of concern. The data in table 7-1 provide some answers to these questions.

At all sites and for all units, few children were said to be in immediate danger (range-11%, Catholic Charities control to 14%, West Virginia control: there were no instances of immediate danger in WV experimental unit cases). Likewise, the percentage of children taken into protective custody or placed in foster care was small relative to the percentage left in their own homes.

There was a slight but nonsignificant difference between units at Catholic Charities. A greater percentage of children served by control staff was taken into protective custody (26%) compared to 14 percent of those served by experimental workers. Likewise, out-of-home placements were made for 24 percent of the control unit youngsters versus 11 percent of those in the caseloads of experimental workers.

The court was petitioned for a greater percentage of control cases at Catholic Charities (21% compared to 12% in experimental) and in the WVDOW

TABLE 7-1.   Percentage of Children by Decision Outcomes for Five Decisions

| Decision | Catholic Charities[a] | | West Virginia | | IDCFS |
	Exp.	Cont.	Exp.	Cont.	Exp.
ID					
Yes	12%	11%		14%	12%
No	88%	89%	100%	86%	88%
AT HOME	86%	74%	100%	87%	93%
PROT. CUST.	14%	26%		13%	7%
PC					
Yes	12%	21%		13%	[b]
No	88%	79%	100%	87%	
CE					
Yes	54%	53%	14%	20%	45%
No	46%	47%	86%	80%	41%[c]
FC					
Yes	11%	24%	13%	25%	[b]
No	89%	76%	87%	75%	

[a] Includes data for both intake and service units.
[b] Decision not considered by workers in the intake unit.
[c] 14% of the cases were transferred to a geographic team to complete the investigation. We do not have information regarding whether there was credible evidence.

where petitions were filed for 13 percent of the control cases and for none of those in experimental.

As previously reported, there was a determination of credible evidence on a very small minority of cases in West Virginia (14% experimental and 20% control). In Illinois, credible evidence was found for approximately half of all cases at both the voluntary agency (54% experimental and 53% control) and at the public agency where a positive finding was made for 45 percent of the cases.[3]

Worker Satisfaction

Workers testing the decision-making procedures were asked to rate them on two dimensions relative to their usual manner of making decisions: first, they were asked whether they found the procedures very helpful, helpful, of marginal help, or not helpful. Secondly, we asked whether they were very satisfied, satisfied, unsatisfied, or very unsatisfied with this approach to decision making. Control workers were asked to rate their degree of satisfaction with their current approach to decision making. Across test sites, 95 percent of the responses from control unit workers fell into the satisfied category. Experimental workers' ratings of helpfulness and satisfaction appear in table 7-2.

Overall, workers rated the decision-making procedures as helpful and expressed satisfaction with their use. The highest ratings were given by staff in the voluntary agency, followed by those in West Virginia and, lastly, by IDCFS workers. Relative to their colleagues in control units, 95 percent of whose ratings fell into the category of satisfied, 3 percent of the IDCFS staff, 19 percent of those at Catholic Charities, and 16 percent in West Virginia reported being very satisfied. Fifteen percent of the ratings from IDCFS staff and 13 percent from West Virginia said that the procedures were of marginal help and 25 percent of the ratings from the former agency and 4 percent from the latter gave unsatisfactory ratings.

Summary

The use of structured decision-making procedures results in a statistically significant level of inter-judge agreement for all decisions that we tested. Moreover, clear direction regarding data to be gathered for each decision and clear rules for using information to select final options results in considerable time savings for staff. There were few recidivist cases at any site and

TABLE 7-2. Percentage of Experimental Unit Worker Ratings of Decision Making Procedures on Dimensions of Helpfulness and Satisfaction

	Very Helpful	*Helpful*	*Helpfulness* *Marginally Helpful*	*Not Helpful*
IDCFS	1%	84%	15%	
Catholic Charities	24%	76%		
West Virginia	18%	69%	13%	

	Very Satisfied	*Satisfied*	*Satisfaction* *Unsatisfied*	*Very Unsatisfied*
IDCFS	3%	72%	25%	
Catholic Charities	19%	81%		
West Virginia	16%	80%	4%	

no significant differences between experimental and control units on this dimension.

Regardless of the site or the unit, only a minority of children were said to be in immediate danger, very few were taken into protective custody or placed in out-of-home care, and the filing of court petitions was rare. At IDCFS and Catholic Charities a finding of credible evidence was made for approximately one-half of all cases. In West Virginia, however, such a finding was made for very few cases—20 percent in control and 14 percent in experimental units.

Ninety-five percent of control staff reported that they were satisfied with their approach to decision making. Between 75 percent and 100 percent of the experimental staff reported being very satisfied or satisfied with the procedures tested and between 85 percent and 100 percent found them very helpful or helpful.

A Search for Predictor Variables

We wanted to know whether there were any relationships between case characteristics or worker characteristics and differential outcomes for children. However, the numbers of children who were in immediate danger, those taken into protective custody or placed in foster home care, or those on whose behalf a court petition was filed (see table 7-1) are too small for a statistical analysis of the relationship between these outcomes and case or worker characteristics. (This is not true for cases where there was credible evidence of maltreatment which is discussed later.)

Unable to apply statistical methods for analysis, we did review our data with several questions in mind: first, were there trends that we could describe? For example, were children who were in immediate danger also taken into protective custody and placed in out-of-home care? Was there likely to be a finding of credible evidence for these cases and were court petitions filed? Or, were decisions to take protective custody and to place children out of their own homes random events, each unpredictable from a previous action? The second set of questions asked whether there were consistencies in case characteristics and outcomes. Were the children who were in immediate danger or those taken into protective custody alike in allegations reported, source of the report, age of the child, number of children in their families, and family composition? As regards the workers, we wanted to know whether cases where credible evidence was found and protective custody taken were managed by a subset of all workers or by different staff. If the former, did the workers differ in years of experience or education from the universe who participated in the project?

Bear in mind that we are looking at a very small number of children: twenty in all. There were seven each in experimental and control units at Catholic Charities, four from the IDCFS, and two in West Virginia control. None of the children in the experimental unit in WV were in immediate danger nor were any children taken into protective custody. We made the following observations.

As regards the first question, there were no trends in the IDCFS sample. Only two of the four children who were in immediate danger were taken into protective custody. There was a determination of credible evidence for only one of these youngsters. As previously reported, we do not know the status of these children as regards foster home placement.

The picture was somewhat different for Catholic Charities and West Virginia cases. At Catholic Charities, all seven of the control unit children who were in immediate danger were taken into protective custody and for all there was a finding of maltreatment. Six of these children were subsequently placed in foster homes and court petitions were filed. Five of the seven children served by experimental unit workers who were in immediate danger were taken into protective custody, for all there was a finding of credible evidence and three were later placed in foster homes and court petitions were filed.

Likewise, both of the children in West Virginia who were in immediate danger were placed in protective custody, later placed in foster care, and for both there was a finding of maltreatment. To summarize, across sites and units, 20 children were said to be in immediate danger, 16 of these youngsters were taken into protective custody. There was finding of credible evidence for 15 of the children and of those on whom we have information, 11 were subsequently placed in foster homes.

These data should be interpreted with caution. We are reporting on a very small number of cases. In addition, the trend we have described for Catholic Charities and West Virginia was not observed in the Illinois public agency. And, as the data in table 7-1 show, as one moves up the decision chain from questions of immediate danger to those involving protective custody and credible evidence, the percentage of children taken into protective care or for whom credible evidence of maltreatment is found increases. Future research may show that there is a strong relationship between the decision to place children out of their own homes and a prior determination of immediate danger, placement in protective custody, and a finding of credible evidence. But, these data suggest that there are other, as yet unidentified, variables influencing the decision chain.

Across sites and units, the cases of 18 of the 20 children who were in immediate danger were new to the agencies at the time the report was received. Here, all similarities end. Within agencies, cases were managed by different workers whose academic credentials varied (BA in the humanities to MSW.) as did their years of experience in child welfare (range = 6 months to 10 years). The reporting sources encompassed all possibilities from anonymous callers to police and hospital personnel and the allegations ranged from unspecified neglect to sexual abuse. Newborns were as likely to be in immediate danger and taken into protective custody as were 10-year-olds. Almost equal percentage of children came from single-parent families as did those from two-parent families, the children were as apt to be boys as girls, to have one or six siblings, and to be black or white.

Whether there is a predictable relationship between determination of immediate danger and the probability of being taken into protective custody, a finding of credible evidence and placement out of the home is worth exploring in future research. Since the first two decisions in this chain are made within 24 hours of the time a report is received, the ability to predict the likelihood that credible evidence of abuse or neglect will be established and cases opened for services should have important implications for resource allocation and for preparing parents and children for services.

A Finding of Credible Evidence

As with other case outcomes, we wanted to know whether there was any relationship between case characteristics or worker characteristics and a finding of credible evidence. As the data in table 7-1 show, evidence of maltreatment was found for approximately 50 percent of all Illinois cases. West Virginia, where a determination of credible evidence was made for 14 percent of experimental cases and for 20 percent of those in control, stands in sharp contrast.

Using the case as the unit for analysis,[4] we sought to answer the question whether there was any relationship between nine case characteristics and three characteristics of workers and this outcome using Guttman's Lambda as a measure of association.[5]

The case characteristics we looked at were: case status at time of referral,[6] whether there were prior reports of abuse or neglect, the source of the referral, the allegations, the age, sex, and race of the child, number of children in the family, and family composition. Characteristics of workers were degree held (BA, BSW, and MSW), length of time practiced in child welfare, and length of time in current position.

The strongest associations found were between referral source and a finding of credible evidence where cases referred by social service agencies (for the IDCFS sample), by police (for Catholic Charities control), and by hospital personnel (experimental and control at Catholic Charities) were more likely to have a determination of credible evidence made than when cases were referred by other sources. But the association was weak. Knowledge of the referring source eliminated only 31 percent of the errors in guessing for Catholic Charities cases and 41 percent of the errors for cases handled at the public agency.[7] Associations for other characteristics of the case or the worker did not exceed .20.

Discussion

Two decades have passed since the importance of developing procedures to guide child welfare workers in making critical decisions was first noted in the child welfare literature.[8] Since that time, guidelines for making decisions to move children who are in out-of-home placement into permanent homes have been developed and tested in permanency planning projects which took service-planning decisions as their point of departure for articulating a framework for selection of options.[9] The work reported here is complementary to that of earlier permanency planning projects. In developing a decision-making framework we began with initial intake decisions and concluded with decisions involved in service planning. Interfacing our procedures for decision making with those developed by others should provide guidance for making all choices from the point of initial contact with clients through to case termination.

The harmony between the procedures developed and tested in the Illinois/West Virginia project and those developed and tested in the State of Oregon and in Alameda County goes beyond the identification of procedures for making a sequence of decisions. The work of these projects rests on a common set of values regarding family privacy, the right of families to be free from outside intrusion as well as the right of family members to be participants in making those decisions that affect their lives. Upholding these values requires that coercive state intervention be kept to a minimum, occurring only when there is evidence that children are in danger, not solely because parents behave in ways that are distasteful to the community. Moreover, the work of these projects explicity recognizes the limits of knowledge as regards making the long-range predictions called for by the best interest of the child test. Finally, these projects have in common a concern with limiting individual subjectivity and bias in the choice process. Accomplishing this required identification of the data base necessary for making decisions and that these data be observable and measurable.

Some professionals will no doubt take issue with a structured approach to decision making, arguing that it reduces worker autonomy. But, the use of structured decision-making procedures can be justified with reference to the profession and to the clients that are served. Professional credibility rests partly on a claim to unique expertise. Allowing personal values and biases to influence decisions made by child welfare workers greatly undermines a claim to professional status.

The use of structured decision-making procedures reduces the likelihood that individual biases will overly influence the process of selecting options. This is clear from our reliability data. It is important to bear in mind that using a structured approach to decision making was satisfactory to participating staff.

Accountability to clients, agency administrators, and the public who funds child welfare programs is another aspect of professionalism. Achieving consensus in decisions made and reducing the amount of time spent in decision-making activities are two ways in which accountability can be established. Our data on recidivism and decision outcomes (table 7-1) shows that there were no costs to families whose workers used the approach to decision making being tested. But, if costs were evaluated with reference to outcomes reported, there were none to clients whose workers used their traditional approach to making decisions. The percentage of children said to be in immediate danger, those left at home compared to those taken into protective custody or foster home care, for example, were similar within and across test sites. This suggests that workers serving control group client use a purposeful, albeit unarticulated, approach to selecting options.

In this regard, a number of staff in experimental units told us that many elements of the decision-making framework that we tested reflected issues they frequently considered during the choice process as well as their general way of viewing information. This position was stated succinctly by several staff persons who noted that the decision-making framework used during the project "concretized their gut-level feelings." Such concretization is not easily dismissed. Staff noted further that having decision-making criteria and rules spelled out in concrete terms, with reference to observable phenomena, gave them a source of support when they were called upon to justify their choices. However, the significant savings in time for experimental when compared to control staff indicate that the methods used during the project did more than simply codify a preexisting method of selection.

The differences in time that Catholic Charities service workers spent in decision-making activities when cases came from an experimental compared to a control worker and their evaluation of material from experimental staff as more useful than material they usually received when cases were transferred is especially significant. Exchanging information with others within and outside of one's own agency is a normative aspect of child welfare practice. But, if data are not readily interpretable to the person receiving it, time is wasted clarifying information, gathering additional data (much of which may be redundant of that gathered by intake staff), and in consultation. It is likely that service provision will be interrupted because of time spent in these activities and that clients will be subjected to repetitive data-gathering tasks.

Any procedure that will save workers time and increase reliability and the likelihood of providing uninterrupted service without being costly in regard to outcomes and reduce the chances that clients will be subjected to repetitive data gathering is worthwhile in its own right.

There are additional aspects of accountability to clients, many of which have to do with the legal framework that is growing around child welfare practice. This subject will be discussed in depth in the next chapter.

Limitations of the Study

The Illinois/West Virginia project suffers from four limitations: the lack of a control group in the Illinois public agency, our lack of success in obtaining data from service staff in that agency, limited follow up of cases, and the absence of on-site reliability tests.

The problems that could have resulted from the first concern are somewhat militated by having had control groups at Catholic Charities and in West Virginia. Moreover, the comparability of data reported by staff in the two public agencies further reduces the difficulties that we would otherwise have faced. Still, from a purist standpoint, there is no substitute for a directly comparable control group.

We have described the positive effects on service staff in the voluntary agency of having received cases from experimental intake workers. These results would have been greatly enhanced had service workers in the public agency provided data that we could have used.

Whether the findings reported would have held true for the public setting is a question that we cannot address. Structural differences between the public and voluntary agencies—the fact that the former is a large bureaucracy where direct communication between staff is limited, causing workers to place greater reliance on written communication than is the case in the smaller agency—would have made these data very useful for administrators of large, bureaucratically structured agencies.

Data gathered during a longer follow-up period could have been instructive. While there were no differences in outcomes between experimental and control units (e.g., with regard to children in immediate danger or the percentages of children taken into protective custody), it would be important to know whether outcomes reported would have been the same or different over time.

A longer follow-up period might have cast some light on the question of whether the investigative or service models we have discussed make any differences with regard to case outcomes. Had we followed cases through to their termination some differences which might serve as a basis for recommending one approach over another might have been observed. Whether families whose workers have a service orientation from the point of initial contact when compared to those whose entry into services begins with an investigatory worker differ in sustaining involvement in case planning and service delivery and whether they differ in recurrence of maltreatment or satisfaction with services are important questions but they are unanswerable from our data.

Finally, on-site reliability testing, using actual case records as the basis for testing, would have increased our confidence in the ability of workers to reach consensus decisions using the procedures tested.

Notes and References

1. That workers use an unstructured approach to decision making is clear from survey data collected prior to the start of the field test. See chapter 8, pages 185 through 186.

2. Recidivism was defined as a second or third report of maltreatment subsequent to completion of the investigation.

3. Fourteen percent of the children served at the IDCFS were transferred from intake units to geographic teams for completion of the investigation. We do not have information regarding a final determination for these cases.

4. At IDCFS there was finding of credible evidence for 19 of 42 children (45%). At Catholic Charities, for 26 out of 48 experimental unit children (54%) and for 25 of 47 children in control (53%) credible evidence was found. West Virginia is excluded from this discussion since evidence of maltreatment was found for only two experimental unit cases and for three in control.

5. Our dependent variable is nominal as are 8 of the 12 variables describing worker and case characteristics.

6. The three status alternatives were new, active, or reopened. Cases were counted as currently active or reopened if the family had received any services from the agency (not only protective services).

7. For a discussion of Guttman's Lambda, see Linton C. Freeman, *Elementary Applied Statistics* (New York: John Wiley and Sons, Inc., 1965), ch. 7.

8. For a review of these studies, see Theodore J. Stein, Eileen D. Gambrill, and Kermit T. Wiltse, *Children in Foster Homes: Achieving Continuity in Care* (New York: Praeger Publishing Co., division of Holt, Rinehart and Winston, 1978), ch. 1.

9. Stein et al., op cit.; Arthur C. Emlen et al., *Freeing Children for Permanent Placement* (Portland, Oregon: Regional Research Institute for Human Services, Portland State University, 1975).

8 IMPLICATIONS OF THE STUDY

In the introduction to this book we noted that the literature from the United States, Canada, and several Western European countries reflects a shared concern about children who reside in unplanned, substitute care arrangements and a growing recognition of the importance of making permanent plans for these children. Focusing attention on finding permanent homes for young people, many of whom experience multiple foster home placements during their tenure in the child welfare system, has been of the utmost importance. But, there is little disagreement that permanency planning must begin at intake. All decisions that are made from the point of entry into the child welfare system must address the question Will the option selected further or impede progress toward permanency goals? Despite its importance, the intake process has, in the main, been overlooked as professionals have struggled with developing and implementing procedures to ensure permanency for children already in out-of-home placement.

The purpose of the Illinois/West Virginia project was to address the need for a structured framework for decision making at child welfare intake. The data on inter-judge reliability show that individual subjectivity in decision making can be markedly reduced relative to the findings reported in previous research,[1] and that significant savings in time can be achieved for both intake

135

and service workers. Moreover, these accomplishments are possible with no cost to worker satisfaction and with no increase in recurrence of maltreatment. It is our hope that the decision-making materials tested during the project, the implications of which are discussed in this chapter, will be of use to child welfare professionals here and abroad as they struggle with issues which must be resolved in order to fulfill the promise of permanency planning for children.

Implications for Child Welfare Practice

A number of changes in the child welfare system were outlined at the end of chapter 1. The framework for accountability created by reform of the child welfare system will continue to grow, exerting a strong influence on social work practice in child welfare. This conviction influenced our work in developing procedures for decision making at intake.

An effective response to systemic reforms will require workers to modify their approach to information management, the ways in which they view and interact with their clients, their ideas about the purposes of state intervention in family life and of their role in this process. These topics provide a framework for discussing project implications.

Intake Decisions and Information Management

The central task of project workers was to test procedures for decision making at intake—the gateway to services offered by child caring agencies. Data compiled by intake staff and the decisions they make are of critical importance. A framework governing future transactions between families and child welfare agencies, the courts and other service providers is established at this time. Information management, including gathering and using data to make decisions, compiling case records, and reporting information to others is central to all intake activities. Information management is the essence of decision making.

Yet, as noted in chapter 2, the sources to which a worker might turn for guidance in making decisions—professional standards, the professional literature, statutory law, and agency policy—offer little assistance with direct application to decision making in practice situations (p. 17). Overcoming this limitation by developing materials that would be useful to practitioners was the most significant challenge for the project.

Accomplishing this goal required more than the specification of decision-making criteria and the delineation of rules for using information. Criteria and rules are necessary elements of a decision-making framework. Their specification, however, is little more than an academic exercise unless one is able to reduce the amount of information that workers gather and affect the ways in which information is recorded.

The quantity of data to be managed had to be reduced to a core set of elements that were both necessary and sufficient for making each decision. Reduction of information was essential because there are limits to the amount of written material that a person can manage at one time.[2] Having access to voluminous amounts of data may be comforting to the decision maker who believes that there is an association between quantity and the likelihood of selecting a correct option, but it is dysfunctional to the selection process. Our ideal was to help workers learn to build an information base in an incremental manner, starting with necessary data and adding information as its salience to decision making became clear. (Our approach to identifying minimum information is discussed on pages 59 and 60, 64 and 65.)

That large quantities of data are an impediment to decision making and that data-gathering is intrusive for clients was stressed during training of project workers. In follow-up consultation sessions the workers were asked to justify the accumulation of information beyond the minimum identified in our decision-making material. Asking workers to indicate the exact ways in which additional information would contribute to decision-making or how children would be placed at risk if decisions were made using only the information specified in the training materials was a learning process for both research staff and workers. Worker input resulted in modifications of the decision-making material. Data elements were added and deleted as a function of worker experience in applying the decision-making framework to cases. Conversely, the dialogue that ensued from posing questions to ascertain the relevance of information, facilitated staff learning to discriminate relevant from irrelevant data.

During training and consultation periods staff development of skills for observation and descriptive writing took place. Inferential recording is normative practice in social work.[3] But, recording inferences rather than describing observations upon which inferences are drawn precludes the likelihood of achieving consensus decisions since subjective interpretation of case materials is required. The importance of descriptive recording cannot be overstated. There is little to be gained from efforts to apply specific decision-making rules to a data base the meaning of which is subject to differential interpretation. In emphasizing descriptive recording we were concerned with the usefulness of written material to the worker responsible for compiling the case record as well as its utility to others who rely on the case record to do their work.

In the three agencies where the field test was conducted the investigation and service-delivery functions were separated. Staff responsible for providing services were dependent, in varying degrees, on recorded information to carry out their tasks. In a relatively small agency such as Catholic Charities, service staff who work the same hours as investigative workers and whose work stations are geographically proximate to those of their colleagues may, if necessary, make direct requests for clarification of recorded material if its meaning is ambiguous. That this occurred is shown in table 6-11 (page 151). However, service workers whose cases came from control intake staff spent significantly more time clarifying data than did staff whose cases originated from experimental workers. (Fifty minutes for the latter compared to 1 hour and 44 minutes for the former.) In the public agency where work shifts differ and where size of the physical plant mitigates against direct contact by staff, dependency on recorded materials increases.

For workers to whom a case is transferred or those who inherit the caseload of a departing staff person, the case record may be the only source of information regarding agency transactions with clients. Whether the contents of the record explicitly report decisions made, the basis for choosing one option over another; whether they describe services offered and outcomes achieved will condition a worker's ability to offer uninterrupted services to clients.

Written material is important to persons other than the initial recorder. Practitioners often rely on their own recordings when preparing reports for the court or for other professionals. If documentation is vague it may be uninterpretable at a later date to the person who compiled the initial material.

Records must be complete in addition to being descriptive.[4] They must contain all of the information deemed necessary and sufficient to reach each decision. To ensure completeness of records we developed recording forms for use by project workers.[5] Each form covered one topic of information such as information provided by a reporter to a hotline worker, a client's current and prior use of services, and a form for profiling family problems. A series of headings and subheadings printed on each form cued staff to gather relevant data.

Eliminating the use of free-flowing case narratives was an objective. Such recordings are often redundant of information in certain areas and void of information in other areas. Instead, a narrative outline with space for recording under each of several topics in which information was deemed necessary was used.[6]

When the project began, we were concerned that staff would resist the imposed structure. There was some initial reluctance, although it was not as great as we had anticipated. Staff referred to the decision-making guidelines and their new approach to documenting information as increasing their confidence in decisions made with specific reference to their ability to defend their choices on rational grounds. This can increase a worker's overall sense of competence particularly in her interactions with the juvenile court.

Significant in this regard is the fact that staff at Catholic Charities whose cases from workers using experimental procedures spent significantly less time in decision-making activities than did staff whose cases came from control workers. Of equal importance is the fact they also evaluated information as more useful when it came from an experimental compared to a control worker.

Recording inferences and summarizing a client's experiences with the use of labels is a form of shorthand that may initially be more simple than descriptive recording. Learning to write descriptively is time consuming. But, over time, inferential recording practices must be costly to staff and to clients. It is difficult if not impossible to recapitulate the factual basis for impressionistic evaluations after initial recording has occurred. High staff turnover creates a special set of problems since a new worker's ability to provide uninterrupted service is partly contingent on his ability to decipher material in the case record. If recorded material cannot be understood, clients may be subjected to repetitive data-gathering tasks and they may experience service disruption. And, the use of psychological labels may result in intervention decisions that favor counseling over practical solutions such as the use of day care or homemaker services. Finally, the use of perjorative labels must result in an overly pessimistic view of clients in terms of the likelihood of their making desired changes.

Parental Participation in Decision Making

Involving clients in decision making is one way of operationalizing the value social workers place on client self-determination. In child welfare, insofar as a child's birth parents are concerned, the evidence suggests that this value may have been honored more in the breach than in practice. The lack of services to biological parents, failure to involve them in preplacement decisions or to encourage them to visit their children in foster homes, and agency policies creating barriers to parental visiting attest to a lack of concern for engaging this client group.[7]

Efforts to correct this problem come from different sources. Child welfare professionals have been forced to reconcile the discrepancy between the value placed on client self-determination with the evidence just mentioned. Fanshel's data showing the relationship between parental visiting and discharge from foster care and his suggestion that birth parents are often the best resource for children in placement have forced this issue.[8]

The juvenile court is demonstrating increased concern for parental involvement. Methods of monitoring agency efforts to involve a child's family of origin are being established. These efforts can be seen in the work of the National Council of Juvenile and Family Court Judges who, in 1982, published a manual which is intended to provide guidance to judges during review.[9] To emphasize the importance of biological parent involvement in the planning process, judges are admonished to ask parents a series of questions regarding their involvement in case planning. Whether parents understand the case plan, agree with its goals and objectives, have had sufficient time to comply with the requirements set forth in the plan, and what benefits they have derived from the plan are only some of the issues judges are being asked to determine.[10]

The heaviest burden for involving biological parents falls on intake workers—not only protective service personnel but all staff who perform a gatekeeping function. The intake process is a transition point where families move from the private to the public sphere, giving up a measure of autonomy in exchange for some form of assistance. At intake, the ground rules for subsequent parental involvement are established. Practitioners explicitly inform families of agency or court expectations such as requirements for participation in service programs when intervention is involuntary and visiting of children in foster care. By their actions, they indicate the breadth and substance of parental involvement.

In developing our approach to decision making we were concerned with questions of how worker activities during the intake process could facilitate or impede involvement of this client group. Two closely related issues were addressed during training and throughout the field test. The manner in which staff record information was the first issue. The information that workers focus on during interviews and periods of observation (e.g., the data base they choose to record) was the second concern.

The issue of recording practices is straightforward. If clients are to be active participants in decision making they must be able to comprehend the issues at hand. Comprehension is partly a function of the manner in which information is recorded. It is unlikely that a client will be able to participate in decision making when the information base for selecting options consists largely of professional jargon, the meaning of which is debatable among professionals and uninterpretable to lay people. Thus, descriptive recording is seen as a minimum condition for involving clients in the choice process.

The material that is recorded is as important as the manner of recording. The bleak picture presented by an emphasis on family problems to the neglect of strengths is not likely to encourage workers to make efforts to involve parents nor parents to take an active role in planning. However, encouraging staff to present a balanced view of family life requires modifications in the ways in which workers perceive the antecedents of maltreatment.

In chapter 3 we reviewed a series of strategies that influence the decision-making behavior of individuals. Use of two decisional strategies, the representative heuristic and the availability heuristic, are salient to this discussion. The representative heuristic is used to facilitate assignment of information to categories. Assignment is based upon similarities between the subject or object to be assigned and one's cognitive representations of that subject or object.

The concept of the representative heuristic draws attention to the fact that a finite number of input variables will be selected in any situation and used to decide whether a family fits the category of abusive or nonabusive, neglectful or not neglectful. Screening one's environment by selecting certain data for consideration and rejecting other data is necessary in order to manage the amount of competing stimuli in any setting. A problem exists if the worker's orientation guiding the selection of data is one-sided.

If maltreatment is viewed as as a function of individual pathology rather than being caused by the interaction of personal and environmental factors, input variables which support an hypothesis of pathology are likely to receive the greatest attention. Indicators of strengths are apt to be screened out. The predictions that follow are likely to fit stereotypical expectations of the class to which the family is assigned. Factors which might lead to alternative interpretations may exist, but may not be observed.

The availability heuristic draws attention to two sources of difficulty for the decision maker. It is axiomatic to state that information that is available in memory will affect worker judgment. The problem lies in recognizing that a worker's reservoir of information is likely to be disproportionately negative since theories of human behavior that prevail in social work education strongly emphasize pathology.[11] Secondly, there is an association between the vividness of information and the retrieval of data from memory. Extremely negative cases of child abuse, about which workers are more likely to have information than cases where outcomes are positive, will be readily available for retrieval from memory, hence, more likely to influence the decision making process. Vividness of information also influences the weights that are assigned to data. More negative information is likely to be assigned greater weight than less negative information.[12]

During training sessions and follow-up consultations efforts were made to help workers balance their problem focus with an appreciation of family strengths. Several strategies were used to accomplish this. The first, more general approach, involved review of research findings and the literature on family violence which illustrates the extent to which physical punishment of children is normative behavior in American society. Our purpose was not to sanction the use of violence as a tactic for conflict resolution. Rather, it was to illustrate the vulnerability of a majority of American families to allegations of child abuse.

For example, between 84 percent and 97 percent of all parents in the United States employ corporal methods to punish their children some of the time.[13] Corporal punishment of children in schools has been sanctioned by the U.S. Supreme Court.[14] The greatest majority of abused children suffer limited physical harm and require no medical attention.[15] We are not saying that the harms suffered by these children are always inflicted in the context of disciplinary action. But, discipline of children accounts for a substantial percentage of cases here and abroad.[16] Data compiled by the American Humane Association during 1978 show that 40 percent of the 191,739 reports of maltreatment received from the 50 states, the District of Columbia, and two U.S. territories were confirmed. In 25 percent of the confirmed cases, loss of control during discipline was reported as causal to the injuries. Kadushin, discussing a sample of abused children in Wisconsin and considering the methods used to inflict injury on children, reports that parents usually use punitive methods more closely akin to forms of physical punishment generally accepted for use in child-rearing in our society.[17] Add to this the fact that 50 percent of all cases of neglect involve matters of nonsupervision[18] and it becomes difficult to sustain a belief that the actions we view as child maltreatment constitute an extreme form of deviant behavior. Familiarity with these data and an appreciation of their implications for protective services can help workers to understand why research has shown that families who mistreat their children do not differ significantly from the average.[19]

It is also important that staff understand that much of the literature on the etiology of maltreatment is based on data from clinical case studies.[20] Data generated from clinical work has limited generalizability. For example, it has been our experience that many workers interpret the clinical data suggesting an association between having been abused as a child and the likelihood of abusing one's own child in causal terms. Moreover, few staff are familiar with the mounting evidence that contradicts this view.[21] And, few staff understand that the critical question for clinical decision making is What are the learning experiences that intervene between childhood and adulthood that predispose some adults to model their child-rearing practices on those used by their own parents while others adopt alternative methods of raising their children?

Staff must develop skills for identifying family strengths, which include a family's own resources such as relatives who can provide respite from ongoing child care or aid in the development of child care skills. Identification of strengths often requires special efforts by workers who must arrange conditions that are conducive to observing parental behaviors and identifying assets in relation to specific problems. The use of role-playing during which a parent who has deficits in child care skills is asked to undertake specific child care tasks, allowing the worker to observe and record the steps that the parent can complete with success and the point at which skill deficits are displayed, is an example.

During training and consultation the use of case examples that illustrate how workers identify and document assets, and how knowledge of assets may influence the decision-making process, is especially useful.[22] Agency intervention may be unnecessary, for example, if relatives or friends can offer supervision for children or assist parents in development of skills.

The Purpose of State Intervention

Data reported at the end of chapter 7 indicate that all workers are acting to reduce placement by providing services to youngsters in their own homes. There were few differences between experimental and control groups in the percentage of children taken into protective custody or placed in foster care. This conclusion is limited by the fact that our data reflect case outcomes for the early stages of intervention. Had we followed cases for a longer period of time, different outcomes might have been observed.

Despite similarities in outcomes, control staff spent significantly more time than experimental workers in all decision-making activities. We attribute this difference to the lack of guidance for staff in deciding what information to gather and how to use information to make decisions. Concern with acting in the best interests of the child, given the ambiguity of this concept and the lack of consensus as to the conditions that constitute its attainment, greatly compounds data-gathering and data-manipulation problems faced by workers. We suspect that one of the reasons why staff accumulate copious amounts of information lies in the hope that some of the data at hand will lend meaning to the ideals expressed in the best interest standard.

To illustrate our concern, a brief digression is in order. A year before the field test began we collaborated on a national survey of child welfare practitioners.[23] Our purpose was to learn about the criteria that workers use in making intake decisions. The survey instrument was divided into four sections and a number of variables that might influence decision making were listed in each. The sections covered characteristics of (1) clients (finances and education, emotional stability of parents, and their interactions with each other and with their children, for example); (2) the agency, such as policy and budgetary constraints; (3) the professional; and (4) the lay community. Available resources, decisions made by others, pressure from community groups, and fear of unfavorable publicity were items listed in the latter categories. In total, there were 36 criterion items listed within the four categories.

Respondents were asked to indicate whether each criterion item was very significant, significant, minimally or not significant, or not applicable in making intake decisions. Variance across the 36 items was minimal; each was said to be very significant or significant for all decisions made. Note that most of the criteria referred to general categories, for example, parent-child interaction and child care skills, each of which could generate a significant quantity of data. Ordering the volume of information that would be on hand if data was pursued in each area would be a difficult task indeed. These findings highlight the need for decision-making criteria and rules for using information.

One source of guidance for developing decision-making procedures was the literature in which continued use of the best interest test as a basis for state action is being challenged.[24] We were impressed by the data from longitudinal studies showing the limits of our ability to make the long-range predictions called for by use of this standard.[25]

We were concerned with how one reconciles the contradiction between a commitment to act in the best interest of children with the value that we place on the right of parents to raise their children free from outside intervention when there is no requirement that the parental behaviors that serve to justify state intrusion into family life be shown to negatively affect a child's well-being. Children have been removed from their homes because the parents were not married, because the mother frequented taverns or had male visitors overnight, because the parents adhered to extreme religious beliefs or lived in a communal setting, because the parent was a lesbian or male homosexual, because the parents' home was filthy, or because the woman was the mother of an illegitimate child.[26]

While retaining the ideals expressed in this decision-making standard, it is imperative to recognize that its applicability for decision making is limited. We accept as correct the argument that the state must modify and limit the conditions under which coercive intervention in family life is sanctioned. Intervention must be restricted to a narrow range of situations where it can be shown that a connection exists between parental behaviors and their effects on children in the present or near future.[27] And, with due respect to the limits of knowledge, we must address ourselves to minimum standards of child care, not to ideals whose attainment is beyond current knowledge. The notion of identifying minimum standards of child care below which there was likely to be consensus that a child was in danger strongly influenced our work in articulating the information base for each decision.[28]

We are not suggesting that staff disavow concern for the best interest of children. Rather, the focus during training and periods of consultation was on defining best interest in relation to current knowledge and helping workers to see that their actions must be guided by available knowledge. It is critical that staff recognize that the child welfare system is not benign. In addition to hypothesizing what will happen to children if the state does not intervene, consideration must be given to the hypothetical consequences of intervention. Technology for assisting parents in problem resolution is limited, as are resources such as homemakers and day care.[29] The amount of time that workers have to help families and their skills for offering assistance are also important considerations in making intervention decisions. Risk to children in greatest need may increase if workers do not discriminate cases where need is greatest and limit intervention to these cases.

Society's reluctance to commit resources for aiding families is a further consideration, as is the fact that children have been abused and neglected while in state care.[30]

The Role of the Child Welfare Worker

When we began work on the project we were concerned with the ways in which a worker's orientation can influence attainment of systemic goals. The success of the Alameda and Oregon projects in placing children in permanent family settings influenced our thinking on this subject.[31] Stein's experience as director of the Alameda project and reports from Oregon showed the importance of the workers' acceptance of an active decision-making role in achieving outcomes reported. We are referring to the willingness and ability of staff in both of these projects to make and to implement some very difficult decisions such as those resulting in restoration of children to their birth parents and decisions to move a case to termination of parental rights. The willingness of staff to be candid with parents as well as assertive, for example, by informing them of the implications of their involvement or lack of involvement in carrying out the tenets of a case plan, was equally important.

While it is axiomatic to state that decision making is essential to achieving systemic goals, it is less obvious that workers see themselves as decision makers. In the year preceding implementation of the field test we worked with agency staff to identify the decisions made at intake. We were struck by the frequency with which workers disavowed responsibility for decision making. In response to the question What decisions do you make during the intake process? the most frequent response from staff was none! Invariably, responsibility for decision making was disavowed and attributed to others such as supervisors, juvenile court judges, or collaterals. Other professionals are involved in the choice process. But, attributing so much responsibility to others did not seem realistic. This conclusion is borne out by our data which show that workers were the main decision makers in project cases, with others accounting for only a small percentage of all decisions.

In conceptualizing the role of workers in relation to goal attainment, we became convinced of the correctness of Wiltse's position: namely, that decision making for the future living arrangements of children is the main business of child welfare staff.[32]

This position differs from the view that treatment and nurturance of children is the main purpose of child welfare.[33] For example, foster home care should, with few exceptions, be used as a respite service for families who are experiencing a crisis which prevents them from providing minimal care necessary to safeguard their children. While the child is in placement, efforts should be made to reduce or eliminate family problems in order to reunite children with their birth parents at the earliest possible time. When treatment and nurturance of children are the primary focus, foster care, rather than being a means to the end of reuniting children with their parents, can become an end in itself. This, it would seem, is precisely what has happened. Having substituted treatment for the goal of family reunification, significant numbers of children have been retained in foster care.

A treatment focus increases the likelihood of cases being retained in the child welfare system regardless of whether services are offered to families in their own homes or children placed out of the home. There is no end to the difficulties that many families confront in child-rearing. But there are limits to what child care agencies can do to mitigate these difficulties. Most are understaffed and the majority of children are served by workers who have no professional training.[34] Efforts to assist clients with all of their problems can only result in lessening the quality and quantity of services provided, thereby endangering those children at greatest risk.

We are not suggesting that direct service provision by child welfare staff is inappropriate nor are we suggesting that families be left with problems unresolved. Whether workers offer problem-solving services is contingent on the ways in which an agency defines its mission, amount of staff training, and staff time. What we are suggesting is that decision making for children's future living arrangements is a worker's primary function. In order of importance, workers must select options, formulate the decision into a case plan, and provide or arrange for services to fulfill the tenets of the case plan.

Moreover, we are suggesting that child welfare agencies must be put into the context of a community's total service delivery system and distinctions made between the mission of child welfare programs and other community programs. The importance of this is clearly recognized in the current emphasis on case management approaches to service delivery with their emphasis on service coordination.

Education and training must aim to increase the worker's appreciation of themselves as decision makers and the fact that decisions are made, purposefully or by default. Helping staff appreciate the consequences of failing to make purposeful decisions, highlighting, for example, the extent to which the drift of children in care was the consequence of nonaction by workers, is critical.

Summary

In the preceding pages we have reviewed issues that governed our thinking in developing a framework for decision making at intake as well as factors considered in training and consultation with project experimental staff.

The topics that we discussed—information management, the workers' view of clients, their understanding of the purposes of state intervention, and their role in that process—are separable for purposes of discussion and training. They are, however, closely intertwined in practice and must ultimately be seen as constituting a unitary approach to working with families.

Training of workers to record a finite number of variables in a descriptive manner will yield little beyond a descriptive account of client pathology unless staff modify their views of the antecedents of maltreatment and actively pursue information regarding family strengths. But, we would speculate that staff will not readily accept or be comfortable with the suggestion that they limit their data-gathering activities unless they appreciate the extent to which large quantities of information are dysfunctional to achieving the goal of helping clients and intrusive of family privacy. Data collection should be justified by its utility for furthering attainment of a specified goal and the utility of much of the data that child welfare workers pursue is determined by the state of knowledge at the time. Staff should learn to ask themselves the question How will I use these data? Finally, helping workers develop an appreciation of their role as decision makers and the importance of this role in helping the families served is a central issue for training.

Implications for Administration

A series of worker behaviors that are seen as necessary for reliable and efficient decision making have been reviewed. Gathering limited amounts of information, presenting a balanced view of family life by recording strengths as well as weaknesses, and documenting information in a descriptive manner lay a foundation for the selection process. A structured approach to decision making saves significant amounts of worker time, increases the utility of information for staff whose activities are based on data recorded by others; it is satisfactory to workers and is supportive of realizing systemic goals.

Changes in worker behavior and maintenance of new behaviors are not likely to come about without a strong commitment from administrators of child welfare agencies. In the balance of this chapter we will address ways in which administrators can operationalize a commitment to change with reference to staff training and the implementation of programmatic innovations.

Training of Workers

Our approach to training of project workers was described in chapter 5. Salient aspects of the training format are discussed next.

Training occurred in two stages. The four training sessions took place before the field test (see chapter 5) and comprised the first stage. Subsequently, supervisors of experimental units and their workers consulted with a member of the research staff on a monthly basis. Ongoing skills development and maintenance of change was the primary purpose of these meetings. Our experience suggests that this training format differs from the way in which in-service training is generally offered where outside experts are brought in for one-shot seminars with no provision for offering consultation to staff as they strive to implement new skills.

Our training program was based on two premises. Staff would encounter problems as they applied new approaches to gathering and using information. Supervisors would not be able to provide problem-solving consultation because the procedures were new to them. Therefore, the ability and willingness of staff to utilize project materials was contingent upon consultation to work out problems encountered.

In addition, consultation periods provided the opportunity to reinforce workers for their efforts in using project materials, to ensure that staff were implementing the procedures in accordance with training (e.g., that the procedures were getting a fair test), and to elicit input from workers needed to modify decision-making materials so as to increase their usefulness to practitioners. A final goal was to transfer the consultation function to the supervisor who attended all follow-up sessions and with whom project staff consulted on issues of concern.

The importance of ongoing consultation cannot be overstated. It is unlikely that practitioners will be able to maintain the integrity[35] of a new intervention without assistance. It is more reasonable to assume that staff will stop using new procedures or that they will apply them incorrectly.

Administrators must ensure that there are procedures in place for providing assistance to their staff. In times of fiscal austerity, the funds needed for return visits by trainers may not be available. Several alternatives can be suggested. First, consultation through the mails has been used, albeit in a limited manner.[36] Here, workers submit examples of their work, for instance, a written service agreement, and they indicate areas in which they are having difficulties. The trainer responds in writing with recommendations for improvement.

Identifying a local consultant or a member of an agency's in-service training staff whose skills, while not sufficient to provide the initial training, are more fully developed than those of supervisors or workers, is another method. Such a person may, with limited consultation from the trainer, be able to provide ongoing assistance to staff.

Another option is the use of telecommunications. Training and/or consultation using telecommunications has the advantage of reaching a large number of people without the expense of bringing together all trainees. Several sites in one state or across state lines can be hooked up via satellite with the trainer.[37]

Implementing Innovations

In chapter 5 we discussed problems in implementing the project at the Illinois Department of Children and Family Services (IDCFS). Difficulties in the implementation of innovations is not a new phenomenon.[38] While a research project is not, in the strictest sense, an implementation of an innovation, it can be seen by those asked to participate in it as an approximation to that goal. In the following discussion, issues that we consider central to understanding the barriers we encountered at IDCFS are identified. A word of caution is in order. We did not study the subject of implementing innovations in its own right. We can describe the problems that we faced and by referring to the literature on the subject of implementing innovations try to understand why we encountered difficulties. However, whether the assumptions that we make are correct involves a measure of speculation. We start with a description of the situation in Illinois at the time the project was developed and tested.

The child welfare system in Illinois, like that in many other states, has undergone significant change in recent years. Early efforts to implement procedures for permanency planning (training of staff to formulate written service agreements, for example) were followed by changes in the structure of the service delivery system as the state endeavored to make general improvements in that system and to comply with the tenets of the Adoption Assistance and Child Welfare Act of 1980. State policy and statutes were revised and a new Department of Protective Services was created, leading to subsequent program modifications. A state-wide computerized information management system and mandatory case review were implemented. Change was rapid; planning and implementation of many systemic changes took place in less than three years.[39]

While these changes were under way, departmental practices were severly criticized in a report issued by the Child Advocacy Project of the Better Government Association[40] as well as by foster parents, 40 of whom demonstrated at a Chicago office of the department.[41] The juvenile court was also taken to task in a report issued by the League of Women Voters of Illinois.[42]

There were frequent media reports on the most sensational cases of child maltreatment. Unfortunately, the response from within the department was for some administrators and some workers to publicly blame each other for reported difficulties.[43]

In the midst of this, reports of abused and neglected children increased dramatically, jumping from 11,384 in fiscal year 1980 to 20,475 in fiscal year 1981. It was projected that the number would increase to 27,700 in fiscal year 1982.[44] There was insufficient staff in Chicago to handle the volume of reports.[45]

This was the climate in which the project began. Central administration in Springfield was supportive of our efforts. Letters were written to local administrators and staff, initially requesting that they participate; subsequently, admonishing them to do so.[46]

The situation that we have described is applicable to other states. Studies criticizing management and line staff exist,[47] bad press is not unusual nor are increases in reported cases of maltreatment subsequent to media coverage. Deficits in the number of staff to handle the volume of reports of abuse and neglect is not unusual. Creation of a new superstructure through implementation of information management systems and other components that have been mentioned are the order of the day. What is unfortunate about the situation in Illinois is the adversarial position taken by administration and staff.

Systemic change affects workers and working conditions directly—through training of staff and testing of new procedures, for example—and indirectly by creating an atmosphere of uncertainty in which workers may question the extent of further change and its short- and long-range effects on their work.

The feelings of at least some line workers regarding changes in the agency were succinctly expressed by one staff person who said:

> We have had a new director every other year. (In the 15 years between 1964 and 1980, there were ten directors or acting directors.) Each has their own opinion of how the system should run and everything gets changed. No one ever asks us what we think and no one ever does anything that helps us do our work better.

The Process of Change   Catholic Charities of Chicago was criticized in the Better Government Association report mentioned above. Child welfare services in the state of West Virginia are undergoing significant change as the state endeavors to implement a new service delivery system.[48] Yet, at neither of these sites did workers express antagonism toward administration and they contributed their time and effort to the project. In the following pages, the question Why did staff participation differ across sites? is addressed.

Staff Participation in decisions that bring about program change is said to be a significant factor affecting the successful implementation and durability of reforms.[49] Staff involvement in the decision stages is seen as a predictor of both acceptance and satisfaction with an innovation[50] whereas unilateral decision making by administrators is not conducive to staff acceptance of change.[51]

Whether agency personnel are involved as individuals or as members of a group and whether they are consulted in-person or on the telephone can affect the willingness of staff to change. Stevens found that on-site, group consultations were superior to individual and telephone communications for this purpose.[52] Both of the preferred conditions prevailed at Catholic Charities and in West Virginia where group meetings between research staff, program administrators, line supervisors, and workers took place during planning and implementation phases of the project. This was not the case in Illinois where unit supervisors and line staff did not become involved with research personnel until after central administration had made the decision to involve workers in the project.

Whether an agency is centralized or decentralized can have an impact on staff participation in the change process and on staff acceptance of change. Catholic Charities and the WVDOW are decentralized operations. Administrators and line staff occupy the same building and they work on the same floor. This facilitated formal and informal communications about the project and it eased the process of face-to-face group meetings.

By contrast, administration in Illinois is centralized in Springfield, 225 miles away from Chicago. Centralization increases the levels through which an innovative idea must pass before implementation, increasing the chances that the innovation will be screened out. Highly developed organizational hierarchies hinder the communication necessary for innovative diffusion. Fairweather, discussing the subject of organizational change in relation to his efforts to disseminate a program in state mental hospitals, reports that: In those hospitals that were change oriented, there was a significant degree of upward, downward, and lateral discussion about the decision to implement.[53]

Turnover of Chicago-based administrators, including the heads of protective services, voluntary child welfare services, and the Cook County Chief of the state child welfare agency occurred during planning and implementation for the field test. A new person was appointed to the position of Cook County Chief of Services; however, he was not based full-time in Chicago.

The combination of a centralized administration that is geographically remote and administrative turnover can affect the process of change in several ways. Geographic distance reduces the likelihood of staff participating in decision making and of direct communication between persons who mandate change and persons who must carry it out. It is incumbent upon a centralized administration to identify local staff who can participate in committees charged with making decisions regarding reform efforts and who can communicate with local staff and advocate for change.[54] In fact, local administrators were involved in the early stages of decision making regarding the project and they were supportive of staff involvement.

However, persons who replaced departing administrators were not necessarily committed to the project and did not, perforce, advocate for it. If one considers these administrative changes in the context of the agency climate that we have described, one can hypothesize that the cumulative effects of this on staff morale were not good. This perspective can further understanding of the unwillingness of many workers to be involved in the project.

In chapter 5 the demographic composition of the Chicago metropolitan area was described. Illinois, save for Cook County, is a rural state—two-thirds of the state's population live in Cook County where 72 percent of the AFDC families reside. It is fair to say that the day-to-day activities involved in providing services in the Chicago metropolitan region differ from what is involved in serving families in other parts of the state.

A number of staff in Chicago questioned whether central administration was cognizant of the difficulties that are encountered in assisting families. No doubt they are. However, the perception of staff cannot be dismissed. The fact of centralization, the absence of a full-time chief of services based in Chicago, failure to defend staff in the media, and the decision-making process we have described regarding the project do little to reinforce a perception of administrative support or administrative sensitivity to the problems that workers encounter in providing services.

Loss of Autonomy   Many of the reforms in the child welfare system increase the opportunities for surveillance of staff. Computerized information management systems, external case review, and the involvement of legal counsel for parents and children are examples. Increased surveillance, in turn, portends to reduce worker autonomy. A review board, for instance, may have the authority to require workers to undertake certain actions necessary to involve parents and children in a case plan.

Changes that threaten to reduce staff autonomy are likely to be resisted.[55] The degree of specification in our decision-making criteria, our effort to limit individual judgment, to articulate the basis for judgment when used, and the focus on descriptive writing may have added to staff concerns regarding surveillance and reduced autonomy.

Sieber argues that quasi-professionals, lacking the autonomy of true professionals such as physicians, experience status insecurity.[56] This is a byproduct of the uniformity demanded by large bureaucracies who strive to exercise control over staff behavior to achieve goals. If workers perceive themselves as insecure, changes that had take place in the system and hypotheses regarding those that might follow from the decision-making project could have been seen as further limiting autonomy.[57]

Goal Diffusion is said to increase status insecurity as well as a sense of vulnerability.[58] The goals of child welfare programs are mainly quantitative, measuring, for example, the numbers of children served in their own homes or the numbers placed in permanent family settings. Few would debate that quality of service is important. However, defining and measuring quality is difficult. Sieber's comments on the effects of trying to measure outcomes with teachers could well apply to social workers:

> . . . it seems likely that the difficulty of measuring outcomes would tend to demoralize those teachers who do not possess considerable personal self-confidence. The effect might be to lessen motivation to try out new practices, especially those that involve considerable inconvenience in the initial stages. In other words, a sort of fatalistic attitude may set in because of the difficulty of attaining objective certainty about a particular practice.[59]

The question of concern is Do staff observe or perceive a discrepancy in their goals in relation to those of agency administrators? The service orientation of many people who choose social work as a career is often difficult to realize in public agencies due to time constraints that are caused by administrative responsibilities and large caseloads. If the systemic reforms we have described, including the precision required by the project's approach to decision making, were viewed as increasing the likelihood of surveillance and accountability and enlarging the basis for quantitative assessment of worker behavior, staff's perception of goal diffusion may have been great.

Creation of the Division of Protective Services in the Illinois public agency significantly modified the function of intake units.[60] Emphasis was placed on the investigative function of intake staff with a concomitant decrease in emphasis on this unit's service role.

> Investigators only conduct investigations. They do not provide or arrange for ongoing services, except when emergency services such as medical treatment or foster care are necessary to protect the child. As a result of an investigation, an investigator may recommend to service delivery staff that certain services be

provided; however, the ultimate decision on case planning rests with the service delivery staff member.[61]

This view of the worker's role contrasts sharply with practice at Catholic Charities and it differs from the model governing practice in the West Virginia Department of Welfare.[62]

Motivation to Change   The project required significant modifications in worker behavior. It affected procedures for collection, recording, and analysis of information for decision making. Workers were asked to complete lengthy forms for research purposes with no trade-off against their regular duties.[63]

It is reasonable to question what would motivate staff to participate in the project. Factors reviewed thus far—whether staff are involved in the decision to participate in a project, the manner in which information about a project is communicated, whether there is an internal advocate for change, whether administration is seen as sensitive to the conditions under which staff operate, and whether changes are viewed as increasing surveillance and reducing autonomy as well as similarities between administration and staff regarding goals— can reinforce or impede motivation to change. The differences between the field test sites on these dimensions have been discussed. The conditions at both Catholic Charities and the WVDOW appeared to be more supportive of change than those at IDCFS.

Now, we would like to consider three additional issues that relate to motivation to change. The issues can be posed as a series of questions: Does staff perceive a problem that needs correction?, Do they have reason to think that any changes will be of benefit to them?, and What are the costs of not making changes?[64]

Whether staff perceive a problem that needs correction is partly a function of the feedback they receive regarding the consequences of decisions they make.[65] The fact that cases turn over quickly in intake units suggests that workers are detached from the outcome of their work, receiving little feedback save for those cases that "blow up." Absent feedback, whether intake staff perceive a problem with their approach to decision making is questionable.

We are not arguing that workers must manage all aspects of a case in order to develop an awareness of problems with their methods of case handling. At both Catholic Charities and the WVDOW, responsibility for cases is divided across workers and units. A signal difference in these agencies, however, is that workers have contact with others who inherit their cases and are, through formal and informal mechanisms, made aware of the consequences of their actions. Hypothetically, the worker whose case management activities has negative consequences for colleagues may receive peer sanction and thus be motivated to change. What seems critical, especially in large bureaucracies where size may militate against direct contact, is the establishment of mechanisms for staff feedback.

There is empirical evidence showing that staff acceptance of change is related to their perception that personal benefits will accrue.[66] But, the question What constitutes a benefit? cannot be answered on an a priori basis. Participation in decision making and feedback on cases, for example, may be seen as beneficial by some individuals but not by others.

There is literature dealing with the subject of incentives for public-sector employees.[67] It is not clear, however, that administrators are cognizant of this literature and that they consider it important to develop and implement incentive systems for their workers.

It is our opinion that the working conditions at both Catholic Charities and the West Virginia Department of Welfare—participation in decision making, ease of access to administrators, involvement with cases beyond the exact responsibilities of one's job through formal and informal communications with colleagues and knowledge of outcomes—may constitute a series of incentives, increasing the likelihood that one will scrutinize their work and modify their behavior. Incentives of this type are made possible partly because of agency size and partly because of administrative thinking on the importance of involving staff in the process that results in change.

These conditions were absent at the Illinois public welfare agency. It seems reasonable to suggest that increases in the number of reports to be investigated, staff shortages, systemic changes, and the seemingly adversarial relationship between staff and central administration constitute aversive working conditions. If it is correct to assume that the large bureaucratic structure of the agency acts against informal provision of incentives, then administration must attend carefully to ways of implementing incentives for staff.

What are the costs to workers in large bureaucratic agencies of not undertaking the implementation of change? It is clear that despite frequent memos from administration in Springfield, the majority of IDCFS workers did not actively involve themselves in the project. We saw no signs of negative sanctions being levied for nonparticipation. We are not suggesting that there should have been. Rather, the central point seems to be the confidence that workers had that they could thwart an administrative directive with impunity.

Summary

Social work practice in child welfare has undergone significant change in recent years due to a series of systemic reforms. We have taken the position that workers viewed the Illinois/West Virginia project as a part of this reform effort, having implications for practice that would endure beyond the life of the project itself.

Whether workers support or seek to undermine change is partly a function of their participation in the process through which reforms are adopted. Staff participation, in turn, is conditioned by an agency's degree of centralization. The greater the degree of centralization, the greater the need for administrators to develop formal lines of communication with staff and to identify local persons who can act as advocates for change.

Workers may perceive the kinds of reforms we have described as reducing their autonomy and as creating disparity between their goals and those of the agencies for which they work.

Lack of involvement in decision making, the absence of a local advocate for change, reduced autonomy, and goal disparity, taken together, can be expected to reduce or eliminate motivation to change.

Social service agencies are vulnerable to environmental influences regarding their goals and objectives. Federal and state policies and funding patterns, court decisions, and the media influence the behavior of agency administrators.

Changing priorities creates an atmosphere of uncertainty and increased vulnerability exacerbating the problems that we have described. This knowledge must affect worker behavior as well as their thinking regarding the importance of change.

In Illinois, the Director of Social Services is a political appointment. No doubt the worker who mentioned the frequency of changes in administration and the affects of these changes on staff was cognizant of this. Frequent changes of administrations can have a dual effect. On the one hand, the worker who disagrees with the directives of any one administration can bide her time, assuming that negative sanctions for noncompliance are unlikely, and simply wait for a change of guard. On the other hand, even the most cooperative of workers may become discouraged, assuming that her best efforts to learn and apply new methods will be fruitless if a new administration, in the course of making its imprint on the system, creates major changes in programs and methods of service delivery.

Administrators must be cognizant of the ability of workers to sabotage changes that they do not support.[68] If staff opinion is not taken into account and if administrators fail to consider ways in which change will be of benefit to line workers, they run the risk of creating a superstructure without substance.

Implications for the Education of Child Welfare Workers

The question Are schools of social work preparing students for practice in public settings? has been raised several times in the past twenty years.[69] The evidence presented in this book and elsewhere does not provide a basis for an affirmative response.[70] The continuing trend to deprofessionalize public social services indicates the limited value that is placed on a graduate social work degree.[71]

A main criticism of graduate education is the overreliance placed on training students to assume a therapeutic role in a one-to-one model to the neglect of development of skills for case management, decision making, and for interaction with the judicial system.[72]

All of the skills necessary for practice in the changing environment of publicly sponsored child welfare programs have not been articulated.[73] However, there are sufficient materials available to guide a review of curriculum and for making curricular modifications.[74]

The framework that we used in discussing implications for practice provides one way of evaluating curriculum content. In the following pages the topics of concern are briefly reviewed. Why they are considered salient issues for professional education is discussed.

All social workers, regardless of their area of practice, are information managers. Skillful management of data along the lines discussed in this book is central to all transactions that take place between workers and their clients, workers and collateral resources, and workers and agency administrators.

Decisions regarding the data that are necessary and sufficient for task completion will change over time. Statutory laws and social policies which provide guidance for worker activities change, affecting our thinking about what is necessary. Likewise, increases in knowledge and reconsideration of values in light of changing knowledge force consideration of information issues.

We are not suggesting wholesale curricular modifications each time legislators enact new statutes, judges make new case law, and social policy is modified. We are suggesting that educators must prepare students so that they understand how practice is affected by new legislation and legal decisions. Students must develop the skills needed to incorporate change into their practice repertoire. For example, as we learn more about child development, workers must be able to modify the scope of issues they address during assessment in accordance with new knowledge. And, students must learn both the positive and negative consequences of failing to incorporate change into practice. Certainly, a worker's sense of competence must be tied to her or his ability to reap rewards from the environment. Equally certain is the fact that the larger environment in which practice occurs can be very punitive for the worker who does not have the skills for defending her choices on rational grounds.

Our experience has been that many practitioners do not possess the skills they need to influence their work environments because so much of their training is predicated on assumptions which may be applicable to private practitioners but which do not apply to social work practice in public agencies.[75] Certainly, workers are limited in their ability to effect changes in large public settings. But, they are not powerless. Unfortunately, absent skills for effecting positive change, a worker's major efforts may be negative, taking the form of sabotage of change.

We said that new knowledge can force a reconsideration of values. We are not suggesting that all social work values be firmly rooted in empirical data. Rather, we are drawing attention to two facts: first, evidence can accumulate which suggests ways of operationalizing values, hence more fully realizing those to which we subscribe; secondly, evidence may exist which suggests that efforts to support certain values may be more harmful than beneficial.

Social work's long-standing commitment to client self-determination is illustrative of the first issue. In part, sustaining this value requires client involvement in decisions that affect their lives. As we have discussed, however, viewing clients solely in terms of pathology and describing their lives with a series of summary labels cannot be viewed as supporting this value. There is evidence to suggest that client involvement in social services is partly a function of their understanding of why they are involved (e.g., what they can expect as an outcome of working with social workers and what they will have to do as well as what will be done for them).[76] There is an extensive literature on assessment of client strengths and information regarding use of such information for planning purposes as well as literature on the importance of an ecological view of client problems. Also, there are training materials which can aid in teaching students to write descriptively.[77]

Continuing adherence to the best interest of the child standard as a basis for decision making in light of evidence that we are unable to make the long-range predictions called for by use of this standard is an example of the second issue. While maintaining concern for the best interests of children we must recognize the limits of current knowledge and define best interest with reference to what is possible, not simply what is ideal. The costs to children and their families of decisions made using an abstract value—one that is subject to differential interpretation—has been well documented and demands a reevaluation of this position.

Finally, in discussing the worker's role, we have emphasized the importance of the worker as decision maker. Differences between a decision-making and treatment orientation as regards the effects on children have been highlighted. The subject of worker as decision maker is part of a larger discussion in the social work literature which focuses attention of the role of the worker as case manager.[78]

There is no generally accepted definition of case management nor are there data from controlled studies which would suggest the superiority of one approach over another.[79] The worker's role as treatment agent is deemphasized in favor of brokerage, advocacy, and coordination activities.

Regarding case management tasks, the worker may assume responsibility for assessment, bringing others into the case as needed, and for initial case planning at which point she or he must identify and bring together resources in the community needed to carry out the tenets of a case plan. Coordination, monitoring, and evaluation of services are major responsibilities of the case manager.[80]

Those of us who are educators must take seriously the importance of curricula review and modification. We are of the opinion that the future of child welfare services as a professional social work service is in jeopardy. Kermit Wiltse, discussing deprofessionalization of public social services, notes that efforts to prevent declassification are currently a major concern of the National Association of Social Workers at national and state levels. In his discussion of this subject, he points to the central dilemma confronting those who would argue for reversing the trend to deprofessionalize services.

> The fundamental problem is that we have been unable to prove the greater effectiveness of professionally educated as against the less well prepared staff in child welfare. As social work educators we firmly believe that knowledge is good and hence those with more exposure to knowledge of most any kind are certainly better than those with limited exposure. The trouble is we have precious little evidence that the particular MSW curricula we have been putting people through has made them more effective in the performance of the specific tasks of child welfare. In fact, it has been asserted with some justification that professional education in social work incapacitates people for child welfare rather than making them more effective.[81]

Wiltse's conclusion is seminal:

> I do not think I am overstating the case when I say that unless it can be shown in the decade ahead that social work curricula are in fact preparing people to deliver those services of central relevance to the child welfare field, and that more education is better than less, declassification trends will accelerate rather than diminish.[82]

As Stein suggests, "There will always be persons who are nominally identified as child welfare workers. Whether persons who occupy these positions will be professional social workers as we define a professional remains to be seen. The challenge is up to us."[83]

Notes and References

1. See chapter 2, p. 7.

2. Robin M. Hogarth, *Judgment and Choice: The Psychology of Decision* (New York: John Wiley and Sons, 1980), p. 36; Irving L. Janis and Leon Mann, *Decision Making: A Psychological Analysis of Conflict, Choice, and Commitment* (New York: The Free Press, 1977), p. 22.

3. Malcolm Bush and Andrew C. Gordon, "The Case for Involving Children in Child Welfare Decisions," *Social Work,* Vol. 27, No. 4 (July 1982), p. 311; Wallace J. Gingerich, Mark Kleczewski, and Stuart A. Kirk, *Name-Calling in Social Work,*" *Social Service Review,* Vol. 56, No. 3 (September 1982), p. 367.

4. The poor quality of case records has been noted by several investigators. See Len Trout, "Annual Report of the Project Evaluator," Reno, Nevada: Research and Educational Planning Center, University of Nevada, 1976 (mimeographed), p. 12; David Fanshel and John Grundy, CWIS Report (New York: Child Welfare Information Services, 1975), p. 5; Martha L. Jones, "Aggressive Adoption: A Program's Effect on a Child Welfare Agency," *Child Welfare,* 56 (June 1977), p. 403; Theodore J. Stein, Eileen D. Gambrill, and Kermit T. Wiltse, *Children in Foster Homes: Achieving Continuity in Care* (New York: Praeger Publishers, division of Holt, Rinehart and Winston, 1978), p. 130.

5. Forms indicated data that were necessary for each decision plus information required by agency management. Each time a project case was assigned to an experimental unit worker, she or he was given a packet of recording forms sufficient for the case.

6. Forms used in the project appear in Theodore J. Stein and Tina L. Rzepnicki, *Decision Making at Child Welfare Intake: A Handbook for Practitioners* (New York: Child Welfare League of America, 1983).

7. On lack of services to biological parents see Stein et al., op cit., ch. 5; on parental visiting see David Fanshel and Eugene B. Shinn, *Children in Foster Care: A Longitudinal Investigation* (New York: Columbia University Press, 1978), ch. 4.

8. Fanshel and Shinn, op cit.; David Fanshel, "FOREWORD," in *The Challenge of Partnership: Working with Parents of Children in Foster Care* eds. Anthony Maluccio and Paula A. Sinanoglu (New York: The Child Welfare League of America), p. ix.

9. National Council of Juvenile and Family Court Judges, *Judicial Review of Children in Placement Deskbook* (Reno, Nevada, 1981).

10. Ibid.

11. Even if workers do not hold social work degrees, the fact that many supervisors do suggests that social work education will influence the decision-making process.

12. See chapter 3, p. 45.

13. Richard J. Gelles, "A Profile of Violence Toward Children in the United States," paper presented at the Annenberg School of Communications Conference on Child Abuse, Philadelphia (November 1978), p. 6.

14. See Carol M. Rose, *Some Emerging Issues in Legal Liability of Children's Agencies* (New York: Child Welfare League of America, 1978), p. 4.

15. Alfred Kadushin and Judith A. Martin, *Child Abuse: An Interactional Event* (New York: Columbia University Press, 1981), p. 6.

16. Jan Carter, "Child Abuse and Society," in *The Maltreated Child* ed. Jan Carter (London: Priory Press Limited, 1974), ch. 1. The American Humane Association data are reported in Joan Senzek Solheim, "A Cross-Cultural Examination of Use of Corporal Punishment on Children: A Focus on Sweden and the United States." *Child Abuse and Neglect: The International Journal,* Vol. 6, No. 2 (1982), p. 148.

17. Kadushin and Martin, op cit., p. 108.

18. Leroy H. Pelton, "Child Abuse and Neglect: The Myth of Classlessness," in *The Social Context of Child Abuse and Neglect,* ed. Leroy H. Pelton (New York: Human Sciences Press, Inc., 1981), p. 35.

19. David C. Gil, *Violence Against Children: Physical Child Abuse in the United States* (Cambridge, Mass.: Harvard University Press, 1973), p. 13.

20. This issue is reviewed in Theodore J. Stein, *Social Work Practice in Child Welfare* (Englewood Cliffs, New Jersey: Prentice-Hall, Inc., 1981), ch. 3.

21. Deborah Shapiro, *Parents and Protectors: A Study in Child Abuse and Neglect* (New York: Child Welfare League of America, 1979), p. 34; Shapiro cites two studies where the percentage of parents who were abused as children ranged from a low of 11 percent (Jean M. Baker, "Parents Anonymous Self-Help for Child Abusing Parents Project," Behavior Associates, Inc., p. 69) to a high of 14 percent (Gil, op cit.). As she notes, there is a "lack of convincing evidence to support the intergenerational hypothesis" (Ibid., p. 39, Fn. 6).

22. See Stein and Rzepnicki, op cit.

23. This study was conducted in collaboration with Eugene B. Shinn of the Graduate School of Social Services at Fordham University.

24. See, for example, Joseph Goldstein, Anna Freud, and Albert J. Solnit, *Beyond the Best Interests of the Child* (New York: The Free Press, 1973); Joseph Goldstein, Anna Freud, and Albert J. Solnit, *Before the Best Interests of the Child* (New York: The Free Press, 1979); Institute of Judicial Administration, American Bar Association, Juvenile Justice Standards Project, *Standards Relating to Abuse and Neglect: Tentative Draft* (Cambridge, Mass.: Ballinger Publishing Co., 1977); Michael S. Wald, "Thinking About Public Policy Toward Abuse and Neglect of Children: A Review of 'BEFORE THE BEST INTERESTS OF THE CHILD,' " *Michigan Law Review,* Vol. 78, pp. 645–693.

25. See, for example, Arlene Skolnick, *The Intimate Environment: Exploring Marriage and the Family,* 2d edition, (Boston, Mass.: Little, Brown and Co., 1978), p. 354; Sheldon H. White et al. *Federal Programs for Young Children: Review and Recommendations: Volume I: Goals and Standards of Public Programs for Children* (Washington, D.C.: Superintendent of Documents, 1973), p. 130; Goldstein et. al., *Beyond the Best Interests of the Child,* op cit., p. 6.

26. Robert H. Mnookin, "Foster Care—In Whose Best Interest?," *Harvard Educational Review,* Vol. 43 (1974), p. 185; Michael Wald, "State Intervention on Behalf of Neglected Children: A Search for Realistic Standards, *Stanford Law Review,* Vol. 27 (April 1975), p. 1023.

27. Institute of Judicial Administration, op cit.

28. The information deemed necessary for decision making is described in Stein and Rzepnicki, op cit.

29. Cecelia E. Sudia, "What Services do Abusing and Neglecting Families Need? in Pelton, op cit., ch. 9; Stephen Magura, "Are Services to Prevent Foster Care Effective? *Children and Youth Services Review,* Vol. 3, No. 3 (1981), pp. 193–212.

30. Edward Zigler, "Controlling Child Abuse: Do We Have the Knowledge and/or the Will?" in *Child Abuse: An Agenda for Action* eds. George Gerbner, Catherine J. Ross, and Edward Zigler (New York: Oxford University Press, 1980), ch. 1; *Child Abuse and Neglect in Residential Institutions: Selected Readings on Prevention, Investigation, and Correction* (Washington, D.C.: National Center on Child Abuse and Neglect, U.S. Dept. of Health, Education and Welfare, DHEW Publication No. (OHDS) 78-30160, 1978); Carter, op cit., p. 15.

31. See Stein et al., op cit.; Arthur Emlen et al. *Overcoming Barriers to Planning for Children in Foster Care* (Portland, Oregon: Regional Research Institute for Human Services, Portland State University, 1977).

32. Kermit T. Wiltse, "Current Issues and New Directions in Foster Care," in *Child Welfare*

Strategies in the Coming Years (Washington, D.C.: U.S. Dept. of Health, Education and Welfare, DHEW Publication No. (OHDS) 78-30158, 1978), pp. 61–64.

33. Draza Kline and Helen-Mary Forbush Overstreet, *Foster Care of Children: Nurture and Treatment* (New York: Columbia University Press, 1972).

34. Ann W. Shyne and Anita G. Schroeder, *National Study of Social Services to Children and their Families* (Washington, D.C.: United States Children's Bureau, DHEW Publication No. (OHDS) 78-30150, 1978), pp. 77–81.

35. Ronald A. Feldman, Arlene R. Stiffman, Deborah A. Evans, and John G. Orme, "Prevention Research, Social Work, and Mental Illness," *Social Work Research and Abstracts,* Vol. 18, No. 3 (Fall 1982), pp. 8–9.

36. This procedure was used by Theodore J. Stein and Eileen D. Gambrill subsequent to a series of training sessions conducted for child welfare workers and supervisors in several California counties.

37. Theodore J. Stein and Tina Rzepnicki, "Teleconferencing Training for Permanency Planning," procedures developed and tested for the Region V Child Welfare Training Center, University of Illinois, Urbana-Champaign (unpublished report).

38. See Stein et al., op cit., p. 151; Susan Whitelaw Downs et al. *Foster Care Reform in the 70's: Final Report of the Permanency Planning Dissemination Project* (Portland, Oregon: Regional Research Institute for Human Services, Portland State University, 1981), p. 3.57.

39. A revised child abuse and neglect reporting act became effective in July 1980, modifications in the state's statutes for termination of parental rights were made in 1981, and a state-wide adoption program was implemented in 1982. In 1981 there was a state-wide reorganization of services which resulted in the creation of a Division of Youth Services under the umbrella of IDCFS. This greatly expanded the department's mandate for serving troubled youth. A Division of Child Protection was created in 1981 and the system for investigation of reports of maltreatment was modified in that year. During this time, the ground work for the state-wide computerized information management system was laid.

40. The Child Advocacy Project of the Better Government Association, "The State and Children in Need," (Chicago: unpublished paper, December 1979).

41. *The Chicago Sun Times,* October 11, 1981.

42. *The Chicago Sun Times,* November 1, 1981.

43. In March 1981, The *Chicago Tribune* reported that the Director of IDCFS said that "employees had bungled" a case in which a child had died (March 7, 1981) and an administrator from Springfield blamed workers for the problems in the foster care system about which foster parents had demonstrated (*Chicago Sun Times,* October 11, 1981). Workers, in turn, publicly blamed administrators for lack of direction and for responding to the trouble and confusion created by increased reports by censuring workers. (*Chicago Tribune,* March 24, 1981 and suggested that management ought to spend some time straightening out the management mess in the department (*Chicago Tribune,* March 24, 1981).

44. Illinois Department of Children and Family Services, *Human Services Data Report: Fiscal Years 1981–1983 and Fiscal Year 1983 Plan: Phase I and Phase II, Volume 1,* (Springfield, Illinois: August 1982), p. 38.

45. Ibid., p. 52.

46. The two intake units that participated in the project had volunteered to do so. This distinguishes them from other units who were drafted by administration.

47. See, for example, Alan R. Gruber, *Children in Foster Care: Destitute, Neglected. . . . Betrayed* (New York: Human Sciences Press, 1978); Jane Knitzer, Mary Lee Allen, and Brenda McGowan, Children Without Homes: *An Examination of Public Responsibility to Children in Out-of-Home Care* (Washington, D.C.: Children's Defense Fund, 1978).

48. The State of West Virginia, under a grant from the United States Children's Bureau, is implementing a new service delivery system developed by Peat, Marwick, and Mitchell. See Peat, Marwick, Mitchell, and Co., *System of Social Services for Children and Families: A Detailed Design* (Washington, D.C.: U.S. Dept. of Health, Education and Welfare, DHEW Publication No. (OHDS) 78-30131, 1978).

49. George W. Fairweather, David H. Sanders, and Louis G. Tornatzky, *Creating Change in Mental Health Organizations* (New York: Pergamon Press Inc., 1974), p. 190; Rensis Likert and Ronald Lippitt, "The Utilization of Social Science, in *Research Methods in the Behavioral Sciences* eds. L. Festinger and D. Katz (New York: Dryden Press, 1963), pp. 603–612; William F. Stevens and Louis G. Tornatzky, "The Dissemination of Evaluation: An Experiment," *Evaluation Review,* Vol. 4, No. 3 (June 1980), p. 349.

50. Rogers and Shoemaker, cited in Fairweather, op cit., p. 22.

51. Fairweather, op cit., p. 190; Likert, op cit., p. 603.

52. Stevens, op cit.

53. Fairweather, op cit., p. 85.

54. Fairweather, op cit., pp. 118–123.

55. Fairweather, op cit., p. 5; Likert, op cit., p. 608.

56. Sam D. Sieber, "Organizational Influences on Innovative Roles," in *Knowledge Production and Utilization in Educational Administration* eds. T. L. Eidell and J. M. Kitchell (Eugene, Oregon: Center for Advanced Study of Educational Administration, University of Oregon, 1968), pp. 128–134.

57. It is interesting to contrast this position with worker reports in which they noted an increased sense of competence from use of the structured decision-making procedures since their use provided staff with a rational basis for defending choices made.

58. Sieber, p. 131.

59. Ibid., p. 133.

60. The effect on intake units is briefly described in chapter 2, Fn. 9.

61. Illinois Department of Children and Family Services, *Child Abuse and Neglect Investigation Decisions Handbook* (Springfield, Illinois: July 1982), p. 10.

62. This subject is discussed more fully in chapter 3, pp. 6 and 7.

63. Research assistants who were paid through the project offered to assist workers in completing forms in any way that the workers found useful, including completion of the forms for the worker using information provided by the worker during an interview.

64. Likert, op cit., p. 582; Fairweather, op cit., p. 5.

65. Janis and Mann, op cit., ch. 3.

66. John C. Flanagan, "Case Studies on the Utilization of Behavioral Science Research," in *Case Studies in Bringing Behavioral Science into Use: Studies in the Utilization of Behavioral Science: Volume I* (Stanford, California: Institute for Communication Research, Stanford University, 1961), p. 46.

67. National Commission on Productivity and Work Quality, *Employee Incentives to Improve State and Local Government Productivity* (Washington, D.C.: U.S. Government Printing Office, stock number 052-003-00090, March 1975); John M. Greiner, Roger E. Dahl, Harry P. Hatry, and Annie P. Millar, *Monetary Incentives and Work Standards in Five Cities: Impacts and Implications for Management and Labor* (Washington, D.C.: The Urban Institute, 1977).

68. Sieber, op cit., pp. 138–139; Stevens, op cit., p. 341.

69. Phyliss Osborn, "Client Needs and the Manpower Shortage in Public Assistance and Child Welfare Services." *Education for Social Work, 1962 Proceedings* (New York: Council on Education for Social Work, 1962), pp. 106–115; Ernest N. Gullerud and Frank H. Itzin, "Continuing Education as an Effective Linkage Between Schools of Social Work and the Practice Commu-

nity," *Journal of Education for Social Work,* Vol. 15, No. 3 (Fall 1979), p. 82; Kermit T. Wiltse, "Education and Training for Child Welfare Practice: The Search for a Better Fit," in *A Dialogue on the Challenge for Education and Training: Child Welfare Issues in the 80's,* ed. Ellen S. Saalberg (Ann Arbor, Michigan: National Child Welfare Training Center, University of Michigan, 1982), pp. 5–24; Stein et al., op cit., pp. 135–139.

70. Wiltse, op cit.; Stein et al., op cit.

71. Shyne and Schroager, op cit.

72. Wiltse, op cit.; Theodore J. Stein, "Child Welfare: New Directions in the Field and Their Implications for Education," in Saalberg, op cit., pp. 57–76.

73. To the extent that purchase-of-service contracts provide a main source of funds for voluntary agencies, what can be said about practice skills needed in the public sector applies to practice in the voluntary sector.

74. See National Institute for Advanced Studies, *Catalogue of Training Materials for Child Welfare Services* (Washington, D.C.: U.S. Dept. of Health, Education and Welfare, U.S. Children's Bureau, DHEW Publication No. (OHDS) 78-30127, 1978)

75. Wiltse, op cit., pp. 15–18.

76. Stein et al., op cit., ch. 4.

77. See, for example, Eileen D. Gambrill, *Behavior Modification: Handbook of Assessment, Intervention and Evaluation* (San Francisco: Jossey-Bass Publishers, 1977), ch. 5; Stein and Rzepnicki, op cit.; Theodore J. Stein, *Social Work Practice in Child Welfare* (Englewood Cliffs, New Jersey: Prentice-Hall, Inc., 1981), Part II; Theodore J. Stein and Eileen D. Gambrill, *Decision Making in Child Welfare: A Training Manual* (Berkeley, Cal.: University of California Extension Press, 1976); Anthony N. Maluccio, "An Ecological Perspective on Practice with Parents of Children in Foster Care," in *The Challenge of Partnership: Working with Parents of Children in Foster Care,* eds. Anthony N. Maluccio and Paula A. Sinanoglu (New York: Child Welfare League of America, 1981), ch. 2; Ann Hartman, "An Ecological Perspective on Child Welfare Education and Practice in the 80's," in Saalberg, op cit., ch. 1.

78. Wiltse, op cit., pp. 18–20; Stein in Saalberg, pp. 69–70; National Conference on Social Welfare, *Case Management: State of the Art* (Washington, D.C., National Association of Social Workers, April 1981).

79. For evaluative data on projects employing a case management approach, see John DeWitt, *Managing the Human Service "System": What Have We Learned from Services Integration?* (Denver, Colorado: Center for Social Research and Development, Denver Research Institute, University of Denver, Human Services Monograph Series, 1977).

80. Thedore J. Stein, "Macro and Micro Level Issues in Case Management," in *Case Management: State of the Art,* op cit., pp. 72–

81. Wiltse in Saalberg, op cit., p. 9.

82. Ibid.

83. Stein in Saalberg, op cit., p. 71.

SUBJECT/AUTHOR INDEX

165